YOU CAN AFFORD THE
WEDDING OF YOUR DREAMS

You Can Afford the Wedding of Your Dreams

KAY MARSHALL STROM
AND LISA RINGNALDA

VINE
BOOKS

Servant Publications
Ann Arbor, Michigan

Vine Books is an imprint of Servant Publications especially designed to serve
evangelical Christians.

Published by Servant Publications
P.O. Box 8617
Ann Arbor, Michigan 48107

Cover design: Multnomah Graphics

95 96 97 98 99 10 9 8 7 6 5 4 3 2 1

Printed in the United States of America
ISBN 0-89283-926-0

Library of Congress Cataloging-in-Publication Data

Strom, Kay Marshall
    You can afford the wedding of your dreams / Kay Marshall
Strom and Lisa Ringnalda
        p.   cm.
    ISBN 0-89283-926-0
    1. Wedding etiquette.   2. Weddings—Planning.   I.
Ringnalda., Lisa.   II. Title.
BJ2051.S77   1995
395'.22—dc20   95-16953
                                                       CIP

Contents

                                              * Worksheet

* Worksheet

                            * Worksheet

* Worksheet

* Worksheet

* Worksheet

Introduction

Congratulations on your upcoming wedding! You are about to embark upon the most important adventure in your life and we are honored to be a part of it.

It is our desire that this book be as practical and useful as possible. For this reason we have taken a nuts-and-bolts approach to each area that you will encounter in your wedding planning.

Yet we know from experience that successfully planning a wedding involves much more than making telephone calls, running here and there with a credit card in your hand, hiring photographers and musicians and caterers, and lining up people to help with the myriad jobs that need to be done. Successfully planning a wedding first of all involves establishing a firm foundation for the union that the planning is all about. May we make a couple of suggestions? Enroll in a premarital counseling program. (You might want to ask your minister for suggestions.) Discuss with your fiancé the spiritual basis for your marriage and what part your spiritual convictions will play in your life together. Take time to pray together. And if you aren't acquainted with the Bible, get to know it. It is the all time best advice book for every occasion!

And now, get ready to begin putting together the wedding of your dreams at a price you can afford.

CHAPTER ONE

Starting at the Beginning

Which amount do you think reflects the average cost of a formal wedding in the United States today?

_____ $5,500
_____ $11,000
_____ $17,500

The first? Nope. The second? Sorry. If you checked the last amount, you're right. According to a study done by the Modern Bride Consumer Council, the average couple whose heart is set on a formal wedding can expect to shell out a whopping $17,470. If you are like most brides we know, you are probably protesting, "But I don't have that kind of money! I want a nice wedding, but I can't come close to affording that."

Good news! You don't have to. You can have a lovely, memorable wedding even if your budget is small.

Four years ago, Lisa was given an engagement ring by the man of her dreams. The timing wasn't great for our family, which had just suffered a series of financial setbacks including a fire that destroyed our home. With little money available, both of us (daughter Lisa and mom Kay) were determined that Lisa's wedding would be everything she wanted it to be.

But with each wedding book and magazine article we read, we became more despairing. A nice wedding, it seemed, would cost a fortune, and we didn't have one. That's when we decided that if Lisa was to have the wedding of her dreams without Mom and Dad taking out a second mortgage on the not-yet-completed house, we would have to do some creative planning. We made endless telephone calls, we experimented with every alternative we could think of, and we corralled our creativity and ingenuity and put it to work. Then we organized all the information we had accumulated, and laid it down in a notebook.

Yes, we made plenty of mistakes, but in the end Lisa's garden wedding was beautiful. And we did manage to stay within our tight budget. Perhaps the greatest compliment of the day came when a young woman from a well-to-do family exclaimed, "I want my wedding to be just like yours, Lisa!"

We discovered that there are three secrets to having the wedding of your dreams at a price you can afford:

- Start early and take charge of planning your wedding in an organized way.

- Determine from the beginning what is important to you.

- Set yourself a budget that you can afford and that will accommodate your priorities.

That's all there is to it. Well, almost all there is to it. It does take work, and it does require organization and planning. But we are living proof that it *can* be done.

MAKING A MASTER PLAN

Since organization is the secret to successfully planning your dream wedding on a budget (it is also the secret to staying calm and sane, by the way), let's start by getting organized. This chapter will guide you in setting up a master plan for your wedding. One way to accomplish this is to do your planning right in this book. As you go through the chapters that follow, be ready to write comments on the charts and fill in the worksheets. It may also be helpful to mark specific areas you want to come back to and consider further.

Another way to organize your wedding is to make a separate master plan notebook as we did. This way you can assemble the information that applies specifically to your wedding. We suggest you divide your notebook into sections, then insert photocopies of the worksheets and checklists you want to use. You can add extra pages for your own notes and ideas, and store pictures you clip from magazines, as well as any ads, brochures, and other information you collect.

If you choose to make your own notebook, you will need the following supplies:

- a three-ring binder
- a supply of loose-leaf paper
- twelve notebook dividers with tabs and pockets
- a pencil and pen

We suggest you divide your notebook into the following twelve sections:

1. Wedding Budget
2. Countdown Calendar
3. Wedding Party
4. Guest List and Wedding Gifts
5. Wedding Attire
6. Flowers
7. Music
8. Photography
9. Ceremony
10. Reception
11. Honeymoon
12. Afterwards

Whether you use this book as your master plan or you make a separate notebook, you will find that being organized has never been so easy. So get ready to take charge of your wedding!

CHAPTER TWO

Taking Charge of Your Wedding

The success of your wedding does not depend on how much money you have to spend. It depends on how much care, thought, and organization goes into the planning and preparation.

You don't want to spend your wedding day tired and frazzled, worrying about details and desperately trying to tie up dangling ends. All that anxiety over the cake and food and flowers for the reception, all the concern over the fit of your gown and the comfort of your guests and the smoothness of your special day should be over and done with as your wedding day dawns. So let's get started with that organization.

SETTING YOUR PRIORITIES

Amy had always dreamed of a spring wedding in the botanical gardens. The problem was that the gardens cost $1,000 to rent and she only had $4,000 to spend on her entire wedding. In order to allot one quarter of her budget for the location that was so important to her, Amy wore a white cotton dress she had purchased at a discount store, she carried a single yellow rose, and she planned a simple reception of snacks and punch which were served in the beauty of the flowering gardens.

Laura, in her late thirties, had carved out a satisfying career for herself. "In addition to our families and friends, Ben and I have so many business associates that we really have to include in our wedding celebration," Laura said. "We will never be able to afford all those people!" Laura solved her problem by having a small wedding at her mother's house with only the families in attendance. The total cost was under $2,000. She and Ben saved their money for the reception, which was a magnificent event that cost $6,000, but included everyone.

Hannah, a widow in her sixties, was looking forward to a beautiful honeymoon cruise. In order to afford her dream trip, she limited her wedding costs to under $1,000. Then she booked a cruise to the Bahamas for $1,500. From their wedding budget of $3,000, the newlyweds had more than $500 left for spending money.

Jennifer's parents offered her $10,000 with this instruction: "This is for you to spend on your wedding. If you spend more, it will have to come out of your pocket. If you spend less, you can have whatever is left to use any way you want." By cutting corners, shopping around, and eliminating all the nonessentials, Jennifer got by on $3,000. With the balance, she and her new husband put a down payment on a small house.

"I thought there was no hope of a nice wedding for me," Tammy said. "All I had to spend was $1,200." But she didn't give up. Tammy borrowed a dress from her cousin, her roommate's husband did the photography, a friend sang for the ceremony and another played the piano, she chose inexpensive daisies for her floral arrangements, and she and her new husband had a simple reception on the lawn outside the church with punch, cake, and small snacks that her aunt contributed. The total cost? $1,100!

So what exactly do you want? As you begin to think of what is most important for your wedding, ask yourself the following questions:

What is my vision of an ideal wedding ceremony?

_____

_____

What aspects of the wedding are most important to me? (Such as reception, decorations, honeymoon, flowers)

_____

_____

What aspects are least important to me?

_____

_____

Do I want to have a theme for my wedding? If so, what is it?

_____

_____

What will my colors be?

_____

_____

Are there any specific traditions I want to carry on in my wedding?

_____

_____

_____

As the weeks and months go by, you will undoubtedly be deluged by the advice of well-meaning people who will try to influence you. Some will be blatant with their advice, others more subtle. Your best friend may sweetly say, "Surely you aren't going to wear a secondhand dress? A designer gown may be expensive, but it is *so* much more classy!" Your Aunt Cordelia may state, "You *have* to have a sit-down dinner! You don't want people to think you're cheap, do you?" Or your mother may purr, "I have dreamed of this day for so long. I have it all planned out for you, dear."

If ever you need to keep your head and stay in control, it is now. If you decide on a secondhand wedding dress, that's your decision. Aunt Cordelia is wrong; you do not owe anyone a meal at your wedding. As for your mother's dreams, they are *her* dreams. You are entitled to dreams of your own—especially if you are paying the bills! Lay things out your way, then gently but firmly, with no apologies, stick to your plans.

So what are your wedding priorities? Do you and your fiancé agree on them? Here is an exercise that can help the two of you determine where you want your money to go. Working separately so that you don't influence each other, look over the priority list, then number the items from one to ten according to the importance you place on each.

_____ A stunning wedding ring

_____ An all-inclusive guest list

_____ A special setting for the ceremony

_____ A professional photographer and a complete photo album

_____ Fabulous flowers, professionally arranged

_____ A spectacular wedding dress

_____ An all-out reception

_____ A sit-down dinner for all guests

_____ A dream honeymoon

_____ Money left over after the wedding

Now sit down together and go over your ratings. In what areas do you agree? Where do you disagree? Look for places where you can compromise. With open minds, search out areas where you can practice the give-and-take that will be so important throughout your life together. Continue to work on your lists—cutting and pasting, adding and erasing, discussing and negotiating—until you come to the place where they are in agreement.

Having problems? Ask yourselves the following questions about the areas that are troubling you:

- Is this something that is really important to me, or is it just something others expect?
- Will this matter to me once the ceremony is over?
- Is there a reason why this is so important to me?
- Is there a less expensive alternative I can live with?
- Am I willing to invest time and effort to get this item or service for a reduced price?

Once you have determined your priorities, you are ready to put your budget together.

SETTING YOUR OWN BUDGET

So what is the bottom line amount you have to spend on your wedding? $10,000? $6,000? $3,000? $1,200? *You can't start planning effectively until you know how much you have to work with.*

A lot of people believe that brides who are more established in their lives—those who have been working for a while or who have been married before—have more money to spend on their weddings. That's not necessarily true. With mortgages, debts to pay, perhaps children to support, fixed incomes, and all the trappings of their established lifestyles to pay for—and often no parents' checkbook to help out—older, more established brides may well be on an even tighter wedding budget than many young, just-starting-out brides.

To give you an idea of the flexibility that can be built into your budget, whatever your situation, consider the budgets of Laura, Amy, Jennifer, Hannah, and Tammy, all of whom we met earlier. We'll start with Laura, who had the most to spend, and end with Tammy, who was on the strictest budget.

Laura

	Budgeted	**$8,000**
Ceremony Site	parents' home	0
Invitations	bought discount	100
Clothing	dressy clothes from department store	300
Flowers	mostly for reception	450
Cake	bakery	400
Music	organist and friend soloist for ceremony, ensemble for reception	1,100
Photography	professional	1,000
Reception	other costs	3,775
Gifts to Attendants	shoes for bridemaids' outfits	100
Rings	simple bands	300
Honeymoon	weekend away	500
	TOTAL	**$8,025**

($25 over budget)

Amy

	Budgeted $4,000
Ceremony Site	botanical gardens....................$1,000
Invitations	discount.......................................150
Clothing	discount store 75
Flowers	single roses for bouquets and boutonnieres...........................45
Cake	supermarket bakery......................150
Music	organist, soloist, tapes 300
Photography	professional...............................1,500
Reception	snacks 330
Gifts to Attendants	matching accessories to wear during ceremony 40
Rings	bands from department store......200
Honeymoon	grandparents' cabin 285
	TOTAL $4,000
	(Right on budget)

Jennifer

	Budgeted $3,500
Ceremony Site	home church $50
Invitations	plain paper, calligraphy by a friend 50
Clothing	dress sewed by grandmother.......150
Flowers	bought loose, arranged by sister of the groom.....................150
Cake	dummy cake with sheet cakes 50
Music	combination amateur and pro.....450
Photography	professional portraits, supplemented by amateur shots 800
Reception	catered light buffet 450
Gifts to Attendants	hand made..................................25

Rings	700
Honeymoon	camping trip 125
	TOTAL **$3,000**
	($500 under budget!)

Hannah

	Budgeted **$3,000**
Ceremony Site	bride's home.................................0
Invitations	casual notes.................................25
Clothing	nice dress from her closet................0
Flowers	most from neighbors' gardens 25
Cake	homemade.................................20
Music	contributed by friends.....................0
Photography	professional portrait, many snapshots from friends, formal photographs on cruise 655
Reception	food brought by friends..............100
Gifts to Attendants	100
Rings	no new rings..................................0
Honeymoon	cruise 1,500
	TOTAL **$2,425**
	($575 left for cruise spending!)

Tammy

	Budgeted **$1,200**
Ceremony Site	home church 25
Invitations	discount.....................................100
Clothing	borrowed dress (altered)...............25
Flowers	wildflowers, bouquets....................40
Cake	professional home baker 350
Music	donated by friends 0
Photography	film and developing only 150
Reception	prepared by friends and relatives..250
Gifts to Attendants	handmade by mother 15

Rings	grandmother's ring, sized 45
Honeymoon	one night, one day 100
	TOTAL $1,100
	($100 under budget!)

Of course, in the end the only budget that will really help you plan your wedding is *your* budget. Your budget will guide you through the frustrating maze of endless choices, and will enable you to resist the constant temptations to spend "just a little more here" or fudge "just a touch there." By determining your bottom line figure at the beginning, and by vowing to stick to it no matter what (unless you come into more money, of course), you will spare yourself the shock and dismay that hit so many brides when the bills start coming in.

Will someone help pay? Could be. It used to be that no one had to ask a bride, "Who is paying the bills?" The answer was always the same: "My family, of course." Not so today. Nowadays early, honest talks about money matters are completely appropriate. You, your groom-to-be, your parents, his parents—all of you can be involved in helping to finance your wedding. Your special day will be shaped by what all of you are willing and able to contribute to the wedding costs. For reference, the chart on page 26 will give you an idea of what traditionally is paid for by whom.

Now it's time to put together a budget for your wedding. As you work it out on the Setting Your Budget worksheet (pages 28-33,) take into consideration

- the priorities you and your fiancé have set for yourselves,
- any financial help you can count on from others.

(As you work your way through this book, you will almost certainly decide to change some items and adjust some amounts, so it's a good idea to fill out the chart in pencil.)

Who Pays for What?

The Bride
1. The groom's wedding ring
2. Gifts for bridesmaids
3. Thank-you notes and postage
4. Her own blood test and physical

The Groom
1. The bride's rings
2. The marriage license
3. Gifts for groomsmen
4. Bride's bouquet, corsages for mothers, and boutonnieres for male attendants
5. His own blood test and physical
6. Minister's fee
7. Honeymoon

The Bride's Family
1. Wedding site and ceremony site
2. The entire reception
3. A gift for the couple
4. The bride's dress
5. Invitations and postage
6. Photographer's fee and cost of photographs
7. Videographer
8. Flowers and other decorations
9. Bouquets for the bridesmaids

The Groom's Family
1. Groom's wedding attire
2. Their own traveling expenses and accommodations
3. A gift for the couple
4. Rehearsal dinner
5. Other expenses they choose to assume

The Attendants
1. Wedding attire (chosen by the bride and groom)
2. Their own traveling expenses and accommodations
3. Showers or parties for the bride and groom
4. A gift for the couple

The Guests
1. Their own traveling expenses and accommodations
2. A gift for the couple

How do you feel about your budget? Excited? Apprehensive, maybe? That's okay. Just don't be discouraged. We will show you how to make the most of your money in each area of your wedding preparations.

Hint: Two of the best ways to ensure that you stay within your budget are to comparison shop and to get help from your friends.

COMPARISON SHOPPING

Maryanne and Christine each had wedding budgets of $6,000, and they had set similar priorities for their weddings. Maryanne's lovely wedding fit within her budget. But as Christine's wedding day approached, she was more than $2,000 over her budget. What made the difference? Maryanne started early and shopped around; Christine didn't. "I tried," Christine said. "But I just wasn't any good at comparison shopping."

It *is* hard. Few brides these days have the luxury of unlimited shopping time. Yet the fact is, a principal key to keeping the wedding of your dreams within a budget you can afford is comparison shopping. And one secret to successful comparison shopping is to start early. If you are getting married next month, you may have to accept whatever is available, regardless of style, quality, or price. Bridal gowns are a good example. Many wedding gowns in bridal shops require from three to six months to special order. And making a gown—or having it made—also takes months. If you don't have that much time, you may have to settle for a gown that is not really what you had in mind. **The overriding rule is: The more time you allow yourself, the more choices you will have, and the better deal you will be able to make.**

Setting Your Budget ✤

	Comments	Budgeted Amount
Ceremony Site Site Fee Tables/Chairs Sound System Minister's Fee		$_____
Stationery Invitations Postage Thank-You Notes Other		$_____
Clothing Bridal Dress Veil Shoes Jewelry Lingerie		$_____
Flowers Bride's Bouquet Bridesmaid's Bouquets Corsages Boutonnieres Ceremony Reception Other		$_____
Cake Formal Tiered Sheet Cakes Decorations Knife and Server		$_____

Total Cost	Deposit	Balance Due
$_____ _____ _____ _____ _____	_____ _____ _____ _____	_____ _____ _____ _____
$_____ _____ _____ _____ _____	_____ _____ _____ _____	_____ _____ _____ _____
$_____ _____ _____ _____ _____ _____	_____ _____ _____ _____ _____	_____ _____ _____ _____ _____
$_____ _____ _____ _____ _____ _____ _____	_____ _____ _____ _____ _____ _____	_____ _____ _____ _____ _____ _____
$_____ _____ _____ _____ _____	_____ _____ _____ _____	_____ _____ _____ _____

Setting Your Budget, continued

	Comments	Budgeted Amount

Music
    Ceremony
    Reception
    Tapes/CDs
    Soloists
    Other
		$_____

Photography
    Formal Portraits
    Album(s)
    Informal
    Video
    Other
		$_____

Reception
    Site Fee
    Set-Up
    Food
    Drinks
    Table Settings/Serving Pieces
    Sound System
    Other
		$_____

Gifts
    Maid of Honor
    Best Man
    Bridesmaids
    Groomsmen
    Children
		$_____

Rings
    Engagement
    Wedding/His
		$_____

Total Cost	Deposit	Balance Due
$_____ _____ _____ _____ _____ _____	_____ _____ _____ _____ _____	_____ _____ _____ _____ _____
$_____ _____ _____ _____ _____ _____	_____ _____ _____ _____ _____	_____ _____ _____ _____ _____
$_____ _____ _____ _____ _____ _____ _____	_____ _____ _____ _____ _____ _____	_____ _____ _____ _____ _____ _____
$_____ _____ _____ _____ _____ _____	_____ _____ _____ _____ _____	_____ _____ _____ _____ _____
$_____ _____ _____	_____ _____	_____ _____

Setting Your Budget, continued

	Comments	Budgeted Amount

Rings, continued
    Wedding/Hers
    Engraving		

Honeymoon
    Transportation
    Accommodations
    Meals
    Spending
    Other
		$_____

Total		$_____

As you comparison shop, be sure to...

- **Consider more than just the price.** Jot down such information as how much of a deposit is required and when, and the availability of work samples for you to see.

- **Ask for references**. The extra time it will take you to follow up on them can save you disastrous surprises and disappointments.

A LITTLE HELP FROM YOUR FRIENDS

The most expensive part of almost every item in your budget is the labor cost. Inexpensive flowers become startlingly costly when the expertise and work time of a florist are added in. When professional musicians quote you a price,

Total Cost	Deposit	Balance Due
_____	_____	_____
_____	_____	_____
$_____		
_____	_____	_____
_____	_____	_____
_____	_____	_____
_____	_____	_____
$_____		

they take into account the years they have invested in music lessons, the cost of their instruments, and the time it will take to set up and to pick up afterwards.

As you consider the service costs, you may be tempted to say, "Well, I can do that myself... and that, too, and also the other job." Yes, there is a lot you can do. But please understand: **You cannot do everything yourself.** And, fortunately, you don't have to. You will undoubtedly have dozens of friends and relatives asking, "Is there anything I can do to help?" Tell them, "Yes, as a matter of fact, there is." Also, consider making requests for gifts of time and participation from your friends and relatives. The gifts of talents, abilities, and time can be far more important and lasting than a crystal vase or a set of sheets for the waterbed.

As you read this book and fill out the worksheets, you will assemble a list of jobs for your willing helpers to do. Start now to think about people who might help. There is no better time to start honing your ability to delegate. Is your mom's best friend a wonderful cook? Perhaps she can join the reception committee. Is your cousin a natural at flower arranging? Ask her if her wedding gift to you would be to put together the floral arrangements. Is your grandmother a whiz with a sewing machine? Perhaps she would make the ring bearer's pillow or the flower girl's dress—possibly even your wedding gown. Is your husband-to-be's best friend a photographer hobbyist? He may enjoy snapping casual shots before and after the wedding and at the reception. How about that aunt who is known for her wonderful baking? You may be able to arrange with her to do your wedding cake.

Besides helping to stretch your budget, the participation of your friends and family will bring a special enjoyment to your wedding, and will leave you with many wonderful memories. Nothing will ever replace the moving solo sung by cousin Charlotte or the hors d'oeuvres made by Uncle Albert, the chef.

Who are the friends and relatives who might be willing to play a part in your wedding? What part might that be? This is a good time for some brainstorming. On the following chart, make a list of everyone you can think of who might be willing to help out, and list the job that might be appropriate for each person. Later, when you are ready to plan a specific part of your wedding, it will be helpful to have your list for reference.

When you ask others to help, be sure to:

- **Ask in a way that will allow them to gracefully decline**. There are only so many hours in the day, and some of your friends just may not be able to squeeze in one more commitment.

- **Offer to reimburse out-of-pocket costs.** State up front how much you are willing to spend.

Volunteers ⚘

The more family and friends you can enlist to help you with your wedding, the more money you will save in the end. For each part of the big day, try to think of at least one person you can ask to help.

(Hint: Place a check mark in the margin next to the names of those who have agreed to help you. That way you don't have to remember whom you still need to ask.)

Name	Job Description	Phone

- **Be considerate of your professional friends.** Professional photographers or caterers, for instance, earn their living through their trade. It is unfair to assume they will provide their services for free. Talk about what you will be willing to pay. If the person wants to make the service a gift to you, let the offer come from him or her.

On the day of your wedding, neither you nor your husband-to-be should be involved with any of the last-minute details. Nor should your parents or his, for that matter. (Your special day can easily turn into one of the most difficult for your mother. Less than two hours before Lisa's wedding, Kay was setting up the folding chairs that had been left in a pile on the lawn by the rental service!) You surely don't want to have wedding day memories of frayed nerves, short tempers, and a horrendous work load for any of you.

To protect yourself, your groom, and your parents, think of a close friend or relative you can depend on to be the "manager of the day." This should be a person outside of the wedding party who is willing to take over all the details for the entire day of your wedding—making sure the cake arrives, passing out corsages, providing directions to the dressing rooms.

You might also begin thinking about special people to whom you can assign "honor roles." This is a wonderful way to honor a favorite aunt, stepparent, nephew, or roommate. Some possibilities for honor roles are:

- receiving and recording gifts at the reception
- taking charge of the guest book
- supervising the punch or refreshment table
- cutting the wedding cake

COUNTDOWN

Now you are ready to start the Countdown Calendar (page 38-40.) It is ideal to have nine months to a year to plan your wedding. Six months will be fine, but you will have to work a bit more quickly. If you only have three months you can do it, but you need to get started immediately. And you will have to readjust your countdown calendar and squeeze together some of the suggested times. (Note that some items on the calendar, such as choosing a theme or preparing guest cards for reception seating, may be unnecessary for the wedding you have in mind.)

YOUR BEST WEDDING CONSULTANT

Today, many brides are hiring wedding consultants to do the organizing and planning for them. It is the job of wedding consultants—also known as wedding supervisors, wedding coordinators, or professional bridal consultants—to plan, advise, supervise, gather information, make decisions, place orders, delegate responsibilities, organize, assist, and over all, to coordinate the wedding. But not all wedding consultants are the same. They vary widely in their training, expertise, experience, and in the services they offer. They also vary in the fees they charge.

In considering wedding consultants, you will have four choices:

- a professional consultant
- a bridal shop consultant
- a consultant provided by the church
- yourself

Countdown Calendar ❧

Six to Twelve Months Ahead

__ Set your budget.

__ Choose a ceremony location, date, and time.

__ Find a minister and meet with him or her.

__ Decide on a theme.

__ Determine a color scheme.

__ Plan a reception style and location.

__ Choose your bridesmaids and groomsmen.

__ Start a guest list with your fiancé.

__ Select a dress and veil.

__ Choose a photographer and videographer.

__ Secure a florist.

__ Arrange for premarital counseling or marriage preparation classes.

Four to Six Months Ahead

__ Complete your guest list.

__ Order your invitations and personal stationery.

__ Order the groom's ring.

__ Finalize your reception plans.

__ Make honeymoon plans.

Two to Four Months Ahead

__ Plan your ceremony.

__ Address your wedding invitations.

__ Choose gifts for your attendants.

__ Decide on a floral plan for your ceremony and reception.

__ Decide on a photography plan.

__ Select a music plan for the ceremony and rehearsal.

__ Plan the rehearsal dinner.

__ Order the wedding cake.

__ Reserve rentals for the men's wedding attire.

__ Purchase, borrow, or make small items such as the ring bearer's pillow, guest book, garter, and cake-cutting knife.

__ Enlist volunteers to help with reception, flowers, music, and so forth. List their names. Designate a supervisor for each area where you will be using volunteers.

One to Two Months Ahead

__ Select specific music for the ceremony and reception.

__ Mail your invitations.

__ Schedule an appointment for your blood tests.

__ Apply for a marriage license.

__ Send wedding announcement to your local newspaper.

__ Schedule fitting for your wedding dress.

__ Pick up wedding rings.

__ Coordinate your rehearsal dinner.

__ Make arrangements for after-the-wedding cleanup, return of rented equipment, and transportation of gifts.

__ Confirm that your attendants have purchased wedding accessories.

__ Make final arrangements with the florist, musicians, caterer, photographer, videographer, and volunteers.

Two Weeks Ahead

__ Record gifts as they arrive and write thank-you notes.

__ Confirm your reception guest list and inform the caterer of the number coming.

__ Make a seating plan for the reception.

__ Prepare guest cards for reception seating.

__ Change your name on all official documents.

__ Begin to pack for your honeymoon.

__ Have final tuxedo fittings.

__ Finalize rehearsal details.

__ Arrange transportation for the wedding party to and from the church and reception.

__ Deliver a list of "must" shots to the photographer and videographer.

One Week and Counting Down

__ Make final check-in with photographer, caterer, and florist.

__ Pay ahead for any services you can, so you won't have to worry about the bills later.

__ Pack boxes of supplies for the rehearsal, ceremony, and reception.

__ Have final fitting of wedding dress.

__ Confirm rehearsal plans with minister.

The Day of Your Wedding

__ Eat nutritious meals.

__ Do your hair and makeup early.

__ Relax.

__ Enjoy your special day.

__ Be sure to thank everyone who helped!

After Your Honeymoon

__ Write the last of your thank-you notes.

__ Send notes to those who helped.

__ Exchange gifts you can't use.

__ Host a get-together in your new home.

Professional consultant
$35 to $75 an hour

The most thorough, full-service consultants are independent business people who, for a fee, help plan and coordinate the entire wedding. I mean, they can do *everything*—from renting the tuxedos, to lining up the attendants and telling them when to march down the aisle, to directing the photographer and assembling people for each shot, to making airline and hotel reservations for the honeymoon.

The main advantage of hiring a wedding consultant is obvious—it takes the burden of organization off you. Another advantage is that an experienced professional is likely to have many good contacts. Since they bring repeat business to such people as florists, photographers, musicians, and caterers, they have some clout with them. And if yours is a decent consultant, on your wedding day he or she will make sure everything runs smoothly.

The main disadvantage of a consultant is the cost. Some professional wedding consultants charge an hourly fee (anywhere from $15 to $85 per hour). Others charge a percentage of the wedding budget. (Fifteen percent is common. That means that for every $1,000 your wedding costs, you would need to tack on an extra $150 for the consultant's services.) Still others charge flat fees for performing certain services (such as $25 to help the bride and bridesmaids line up before the wedding, $100 to assist at the rehearsal and wedding, or $35 for one hour of help in selecting wedding invitations).

Whatever a wedding consultant charges, the dollars can add up quickly. Still, if you hate the idea of organizing, or if you just do not have the time to do it, you may want to make room in your budget for a professional consultant. For names of wedding consultants in your area, look in the yellow pages of the telephone book, or call the Association of Bridal Consultants at 203-355-0464.

Consultant Telephone Interviews ❦

CONSULTANT 1:_____

Phone:_____

What services do you perform?

_____

_____

How do you charge? (hourly rate, percentage, flat fees)

_____

_____

How many weddings have you done? _____

*References:*_____

_____

CONSULTANT 2:_____

Phone:_____

What services do you perform?

_____

_____

How do you charge? (hourly rate, percentage, flat fees)

_____

_____

How many weddings have you done? _____

*References:*_____

_____

CONSULTANT 3:_____

Phone:_____

What services do you perform?

_____

_____

How do you charge? (hourly rate, percentage, flat fees)

_____

_____

How many weddings have you done? _____

*References:*_____

_____

Make an appointment to talk personally with each consultant you still consider a candidate. (Remember, you don't have to go for the full-service option. You may decide to hire a consultant by the hour, or only for specific services.)

Bridal shop consultants
Free

Many bridal shops have employees they call wedding consultants. While these people can give you some helpful information, and are often able to pass along suggestions and referrals, they are seldom wedding consultants in the professional sense. The main advantage of bridal shop consultants is that their services are usually free to customers. The main disadvantage is that they will try to push the shop's products, which are usually top-end-of-the-price-range budget busters.

If you choose to go with a bridal shop consultant, be ready to accept information without committing yourself to pricey items. (If you sometimes have trouble saying "no," it may help to take someone along with you who can help keep your feet firmly planted in budget reality.)

Church consultants
Free

Some churches provide coordinators for couples who are married in the church. These coordinators usually meet with the bride several times, help run the rehearsal, and assist on the wedding day. But they do not provide the full service of a professional consultant. The main advantage of church-provided consultants is that they charge a minimal fee. The main disadvantage is that they are only able to help in a limited way.

A church coordinator can be quite helpful in getting everyone organized before the ceremony and down the aisle at the appropriate time. But understand the limited service the coordinator offers, and don't expect more from him or her.

Do it yourself
Free

You have one more wedding consultant option—yourself! The main advantage to being your own wedding consultant is that it will cost you nothing. And with the worksheets in this book, you already have a good start!

TAKE A BREATHER

Whew! You have done a lot of work and made some pretty important decisions. Perhaps you are already seeing how easy it is to get so caught up in planning your dream wedding on a budget that it can begin to take over your life. Why not start training yourself to pause periodically, step back, and remember why you are getting married in the first place? All you really need to get married is a license, a bride, a groom, and a minister. The rest is merely frosting on the wedding cake. What you can do, you can do. What you cannot do, you can get along without.

Remember: This wedding is the beginning of your life together. It is not a social event to impress other people.

It's true, you know. And if you can keep this firmly in your mind, you can survive the stresses and pressures of getting everything ready. You can wake up on your wedding morning calm and cool and ready to enjoy every aspect of your special day. And in the years to come, when you look back on your wedding day, you will have the great satisfaction of knowing it truly *was* your day, done your way, no disappointments and no regrets. What better way could there be to start your life together?

Wedding Expense Record ❧

Item/Service	Comments	Total Cost
Ceremony		
Site Fee		
Marriage License		
Music		
Other		
Other		
Stationery		
Invitations		
Thank-You Notes		
Programs		
Other		
Wedding Attire		
Bridal Dress		
Accessories		
Groom's Wear		
Other		
Rings		
Engagement		
Bride's Wedding		
Groom's Wedding		
Gifts		
Bride's Attendants		
Groomsmen		
Other		
Other		

(To Be Paid By)			Deposit	Balance
Bride	Groom	Other		

Wedding Expense Record, continued

Item/Service	Comments	Total Cost
Flowers		
Ceremony		
Reception		
Bride's Bouquet		
Bride's Attendants		
Boutonnieres		
Corsages		
Other		
Reception		
Site Fee		
Food and Beverage		
Equipment		
Cake		
Music		
Other		
Photography		
Ceremony		
Reception		
Formal Portrait		
Album		
Extra Photos		
Other		
Videography		
Honeymoon		
Other		
Other		

(To Be Paid By)			Deposit	Balance
Bride	Groom	Other		

CHAPTER THREE

When Will the Wedding Be? And Where?

Congratulations! You are already well on your way toward the wedding of your dreams. But you can't go much further until you answer these two questions: When will the wedding be held? And where? You may be surprised at the choices you have.

WHEN WILL YOUR WEDDING BE?

Setting a date for your wedding is no small decision. There are a number of things to be considered:

- Will I choose a winter, spring, summer, or fall wedding?
- On which day of the week will the wedding be?
- At what time of the day?
- How will each of these choices impact the budget I have set for myself?

As you are weighing each of these factors, remember: **the more time you allow yourself, the easier it will be to get exactly what you want for the best possible price.**

Time of year. Are you leaning toward a garden wedding? Then it makes sense to rule out a winter date—unless you live in Hawaii or Arizona, of course. Do you have your heart set on a candlelight ceremony? Then you will do well to stay away from a summer date when the sun stays up later than many of your guests may want to.

As you determine the time of year you will get married, don't forget to consider your reception. On holidays such as Christmas or New Year's you may have to pay a higher price for your reception needs. For example, flowers are more costly during December because of the high demand for them and because of their limited availability. (At Valentine's Day, roses are next to impossible to find at anything but an exorbitant price!) If you look for caterers, you will find them busy handling parties throughout the holidays and not at all interested in talking about making deals. The same is true of musicians, whose prices often go up at this busy time of the year. On other holidays—such as Memorial Day, Valentine's Day, Labor Day, and Thanksgiving weekend—you may also find things less available and more expensive, including accommodations for your guests.

It is true that vacation periods and holidays allow your guests more travel time. But keep in mind that many people will have other plans or family conflicts. You will have to weigh the pros and cons, and also look at your own particular circumstances. Amy, for instance, set her wedding date on Labor Day weekend. Because the only out-of-town guests she invited were relatives, her family planned a family reunion after the wedding.

Suzanne has never regretted setting her wedding date for December 23. It *saved* her money. Instead of paying high Christmas prices for flowers, she paid almost nothing because the church was already decorated for the season. "Poinsettias, evergreen boughs, and a beautiful and stately Christmas tree to one side," she recalls with a sigh. "It was so much nicer than the measly floral arrangement I could have afforded!"

So, again, it's up to you. A Christmas or Valentine's Day or Fourth of July wedding may be wrong for many, but it may be just right for you.

Day of week. There are also things to be considered when you select the day of the week. Overall, Saturday is the favorite day for weddings because it is usually the most convenient for out-of-town guests. The second favorite day is Sunday, but it trails way behind Saturday.

On the other hand, if you choose to have a Saturday wedding, you will have to compete with many more brides wanting all the same services and products you want than if you choose a Friday evening or a Sunday. Nor are weekdays off limits. Some wedding businesses will offer discounts for nontraditional days. For example, bands and DJs often have openings on Friday nights or Sundays and will give discounts in order to fill them.

Again, consider the uniqueness of your own situation. Ellen and her fiancé were married at a week-long conference they were attending for the fourth year in a row. They made use of the quaint chapel on the conference grounds, their decorations were the natural beauty of the stately redwood trees that could be seen through the floor-to-ceiling windows, and the reception in the dining room included more than three hundred plus conferees who were having their scheduled evening meal. All the couple provided was a wedding cake. The bride was radiant in her antique white dress, the groom handsome in his dark suit, and the attendants and guests comfortable in their casual attire. The price tag for Ellen's one-of-a-kind wedding was $300.

One more suggestion: Be sure to double-check for local events that might be scheduled in the area you have selected for your wedding. There could be conflicts that might cause unexpected problems. After Lisa chose the first weekend of

August for her wedding, she discovered that the city's annual Old Spanish Days Fiesta was at the same time. She had a terrible time finding a place to hold the reception. It was also next to impossible to locate affordable accommodations for all the out-of-town guests; every establishment had doubled their prices for the week! On the other hand, after the wedding many guests had a wonderful time celebrating Fiesta. In fact, several families decided to stay on for the entire week. It seemed as if the whole city was holding a huge celebration in honor of Lisa and Arie's wedding day!

Time of day. The time you choose can be an important budget factor. It is much more economical to have your wedding in the morning or the afternoon than in the evening. Why? Because food is the largest expense for most weddings, and dinner is the most expensive meal to serve to guests. A morning brunch or afternoon tea reception can save you a great deal of money. A cake and punch reception following an afternoon or after-dinner-hour evening wedding is also a perfectly acceptable alternative to the high expense of a sit-down dinner reception. Judy told us, "We set our wedding for 7:00 in the evening simply so we wouldn't have to serve dinner."

Consider carefully, but don't be too quick to rule anything out. As we will see in chapter 9, there are ways to stretch those reception dollars.

WHERE WILL YOUR WEDDING BE?

Now that you have a fair idea of the date and time of your wedding, you are ready to consider where it will be held. Most brides automatically think of a church wedding. Yet today many people are opting for less traditional sites. This is especially true for brides who have been married before.

Here are some site possibilities you might want to consider.

Church wedding. The most common reasons so many couples think first of getting married in a church are tradition and the spiritual significance of a wedding. But there are other advantages to a church site. For one thing, the building will usually accommodate a large number of people. For another, it will come equipped with many things we take for granted, but which would otherwise have to be rented, such as chairs, a podium, a piano, and a sound system. Also, the church is usually available at a reasonable cost. Many brides follow their church wedding with a reception at the church social hall, which makes it even more affordable.

Although the cost varies widely from city to city, and even from church to church, the approximate cost of a church wedding site is between $100 and $400. This usually includes the use of the church, custodial services, often the services of a wedding coordinator supplied by the church, and the pastor's time. (You should, however, ask the minister in private about his or her usual honorarium. Some expect it, some do not.) If you are a member of the church, part of this fee may be waived. For very popular church sites, or for historic churches, the cost can run considerably higher.

Before you commit yourself to a specific church, be sure you understand what the total cost will be, and what all is included in that charge. One couple had just about completed their wedding arrangements when the bride received a statement from the church that read:

1.	Minister and use of church	$350
2.	Use of social hall	100
3.	Clean-up following ceremony	50
4.	Wedding coordinator	75
5.	Organist	50
6.	Soloist	50
	TOTAL	$675

(Amount due two weeks before wedding.
Please pay promptly!)

The couple had budgeted $350 for the church. Even that was a stretch, but they decided it was worth it. Now at the last minute they had to come up with an extra $315. The lesson is this: *Take nothing for granted.* Always ask:

- What will my fee be for using the church?
- What exactly does that fee cover?
- What services will cost extra?
- What will those costs be?

Better yet, get everything in writing.

Home wedding. If you are thinking about a small wedding, a home ceremony may be just the thing for you. Whether it's your home you choose or the home of a friend or relative, it doesn't have to be luxurious or have a winding staircase. Nor is it necessary to have a seat for every guest when the wedding is held indoors. Home ceremonies are usually short, and if there is enough seating for older or disabled people, other guests won't mind standing.

Besides the cost advantage, the main pluses of a home wedding are the ease of arranging for the scaled-down ceremony, and the joy of sharing your wedding day in such an intimate environment. The main disadvantage is that you will only be able to invite a limited number of guests.

Rented site. Rented sites offer endless possibilities for indoor weddings. A private club, restaurant, hotel, hall, or any other facility is a potential site for your wedding, whether it is large or small. However, unless you have some special connections, or a particular reason why a specific facility is especially important to you, a rented site may not be a good budget choice. Charges can vary from $200 to well over $1,000, and there may be many extras you will have to rent besides.

Garden wedding. Outdoor weddings can be lovely, and they can be economical, too. In a garden atmosphere, couples are often able to save money on both flowers and decorations, and may be able to save even more by holding the reception in the same place.

Lisa was married in the gardens of a historic Victorian home. The setting was gorgeous, and the August morning couldn't have been more beautiful. One of her friends was so impressed with the wedding that she chose the same location for her own wedding the following year. Unfortunately, that August day was so scorching hot that the guests sweltered. The reception ended early when the frosting on the cake began to melt.

This is the biggest drawback of a garden wedding: the notorious unpredictability of the weather. Depending on where you live and the season you choose, you would be wise to have an alternate plan. One possibility is to rent a tent, but this, of course, adds considerably to the cost. So do the other rentals you will likely need to provide for a garden wedding, such as chairs, tables, and a sound system.

Unique sites. None of these sites sound exactly right to you? Then be creative! Angela, who lives on the Southern California coast, had her wedding at the beach. The dress for the day was casual and the invitations read "Shoes Optional." Denise, who lived in South Carolina, was married on a friend's boat as it cruised on the Atlantic Ocean. Barbara and her fiancé chose to be married on the Montana pasture land they had purchased to start their life together. Heidi's June wedding was held amid a carpet of wildflowers at the Colorado ski resort where she and her fiancé had met three winters before. After a church wedding, Judy and Jason held their reception in the large auditorium of the elementary school where they both worked. "It was romantic because that's where we met," Judy says.

Dream your dreams. Let your imagination soar. Then consider the impact each idea would have on your budget. The following charts (pages 59-64) will help you further evaluate the possibilities for both your wedding ceremony and your reception.

Whatever site you choose, your wedding and reception are sure to be wonderful. And, best of all, they will be uniquely yours.

Have you decided the when and the where of your ceremony and reception? Or have you at least narrowed it down to a couple of final possibilities? Great! You are now ready to go on to chapter 4 and your guest list.

Select a Ceremony Site ✻

SITE 1: _____

Address: _____

Contact person: _____ Phone: _____

Available dates: _____

Available times: _____

Cost: _____ Deposit required: _____

Date confirmed:_____ Deposit paid: _____

Number of guests that can be accommodated: _____

Are there restroom facilities? _____

Is there parking available?_____

Are there facilities and access for people with disabilities?_____

Are there dressing facilities for the bridal party? _____

What accessories does the site provide and is there a charge for them?

__ Candelabra	$_____	__ Kneeling bench	$_____
__ Guestbook stand	$_____	__ Flower stands	$_____
__ Stand for minister	$_____	__ Arch	$_____
__ Seating for guests	$_____	__ Sound system	$_____
__ Tables	$_____	__ Outlets	$_____
__ Other _____	$_____	__ _____	$_____
__ Other _____	$_____	__ _____	$_____

Is there an additional charge for using the site for the reception? _____

Notes:

Select a Ceremony Site, continued

SITE 2: _____

Address: _____

Contact person: _____ Phone: _____

Available dates: _____

Available times: _____

Cost: _____ Deposit required: _____

Date confirmed: _____ Deposit paid: _____

Number of guests that can be accommodated: _____

Are there restroom facilities? _____

Is there parking available? _____

Are there facilities and access for people with disabilities? _____

Are there dressing facilities for the bridal party? _____

What accessories does the site provide and is there a charge for them?

__ Candelabra	$_____	__ Kneeling bench	$_____
__ Guestbook stand	$_____	__ Flower stands	$_____
__ Stand for minister	$_____	__ Arch	$_____
__ Seating for guests	$_____	__ Sound system	$_____
__ Tables	$_____	__ Outlets	$_____
__ Other _____	$_____	__ _____	$_____
__ Other _____	$_____	__ _____	$_____

Is there an additional charge for using the site for the reception? _____

Notes:

Select a Ceremony Site, continued

SITE 3: _____

Address: _____

Contact person: _____ Phone: _____

Available dates: _____

Available times: _____

Cost: _____ Deposit required: _____

Date confirmed:_____ Deposit paid: _____

Number of guests that can be accommodated: _____

Are there restroom facilities? _____

Is there parking available?_____

Are there facilities and access for people with disabilities?_____

Are there dressing facilities for the bridal party? _____

What accessories does the site provide and is there a charge for them?

__ Candelabra	$_____	__ Kneeling bench	$_____
__ Guestbook stand	$_____	__ Flower stands	$_____
__ Stand for minister	$_____	__ Arch	$_____
__ Seating for guests	$_____	__ Sound system	$_____
__ Tables	$_____	__ Outlets	$_____
__ Other _____	$_____	__ _____	$_____
__ Other _____	$_____	__ _____	$_____

Is there an additional charge for using the site for the reception? _____

Notes:

Select a Reception Site

SITE 1: ______________________________

Address: ______________________________

Contact person: ______________ Phone: ______________

Available dates: ______________________________

Available times: ______________________________

Cost: ______________ Deposit required: ______________

Date confirmed:______________ Deposit paid: ______________

Number of guests that can be accommodated: ______________

Description of the facility ______________________________

____

Time allowed for reception: ______________________________

Are there restroom facilities? ______________________________

Is there parking available?______________________________

Are there facilities and access for people with disabilities?______________

Food and beverage option 1: ______________________________

____

Food and beverage option 2: ______________________________

____

Food and beverage option 3: ______________________________

____

What accessories does the site provide and is there a charge for them?

__ Tables and chairs	$________	__ Sound system	$________
__ Piano	$________	__ Decorations	$________
__ Outlets	$________	__ Serving pieces	$________
__ Kitchen facilities	$________	__ ______________	$________
__ ______________	$________	__ ______________	$________

Notes:

Select a Reception Site, continued

SITE 2: _____

Address: _____

Contact person: _____ Phone: _____

Available dates: _____

Available times: _____

Cost: _____ Deposit required: _____

Date confirmed: _____ Deposit paid: _____

Number of guests that can be accommodated: _____

Description of the facility _____

_____

Time allowed for reception: _____

Are there restroom facilities? _____

Is there parking available? _____

Are there facilities and access for people with disabilities? _____

Food and beverage option 1: _____

_____

Food and beverage option 2: _____

_____

Food and beverage option 3: _____

_____

What accessories does the site provide and is there a charge for them?

__ Tables and chairs	$_____	__ Sound system	$_____
__ Piano	$_____	__ Decorations	$_____
__ Outlets	$_____	__ Serving pieces	$_____
__ Kitchen facilities	$_____	__ _____	$_____
__ _____	$_____	__ _____	$_____

Notes:

Select a Reception Site, continued

SITE 3: _____

Address: _____

Contact person: _____ Phone: _____

Available dates: _____

Available times: _____

Cost: _____ Deposit required: _____

Date confirmed: _____ Deposit paid: _____

Number of guests that can be accommodated: _____

Description of the facility _____

_____

Time allowed for reception: _____

Are there restroom facilities? _____

Is there parking available? _____

Are there facilities and access for people with disabilities? _____

Food and beverage option 1: _____

_____

Food and beverage option 2: _____

_____

Food and beverage option 3: _____

_____

What accessories does the site provide and is there a charge for them?

__ Tables and chairs	$_____	__ Sound system	$_____
__ Piano	$_____	__ Decorations	$_____
__ Outlets	$_____	__ Serving pieces	$_____
__ Kitchen facilities	$_____	__ _____	$_____
__ _____	$_____	__ _____	$_____

Notes:

CHAPTER FOUR

Who Will Be At Your Wedding?

Y ou will be at your wedding, your groom-to-be will be there, and the person who will be officiating will be there. But who else will be involved? These VIPs (Very Important Participants) can be divided into two categories: those who will be a part of the wedding party, and those who will be attending as guests.

Let's first consider the people who will be in your wedding party.

THE WEDDING PARTY

For many a bride, the first rude awakening comes when it's time to choose her attendants. Everyone seems to have an opinion:

"Of course you will want your sisters to be in your wedding!"

"What about the groom's sisters? They should be attendants."

"We've been friends so long! Aren't you going to ask me to be in your wedding?"

"His children and your children. They should all be a part of the wedding party."

Yes, it is nice to have family members participate in your wedding. And you will likely want your best friend or friends to stand beside you. If you or your husband-to-be has children, including them in the wedding is a good way of letting them know they will be an important part of your new life together.

Yet as you add up the costs, you will undoubtedly find that the more attendants you have, the higher your wedding expenses will climb.

"Wait a minute," you may be saying. "My attendants will pay for their own outfits. And they will cover their own expenses getting to the wedding." True, yet the fact remains that the more attendants you have, the more of a strain it will be on your budget. You will have to buy more bouquets for them to carry, and more attendants' gifts. Perhaps more important, as your number of attendants grows, the entire scope of your wedding will tend to increase.

The number of attendants isn't the only wedding party choice you will have to make.

"I would love to have my sister and my two best friends from the office as my attendants," Arlene said. "But I'm afraid it would make my wedding look ridiculous. One of my office friends is almost six feet tall and skinny as a rail, and the other is a petite five feet. To make it worse, my sister is more than one hundred pounds overweight!"

If you are concerned about the assortment of your potential attendants, remember that your wedding is not a stage show. The people you choose don't have to be picture perfect. It is far more important to choose those who are close to you to attend you on your special day than it is to have a matched set of sizes and shapes in your wedding party.

When Irene was married for the second time at the age of sixty-nine, she had three attendants. Their ages were seventy-two, fifty-one, and twenty-eight. An unusual variety to be sure, but a lovely group nevertheless, each one important to Irene.

Nor should you allow a person's disability to stand in the way of including her or him in your wedding party. One bride had her father escort her down the aisle even though he was in a wheelchair. Another had a bridesmaid who slowly made her way along the aisle on crutches. Yet another included her brother, who had Down's syndrome, as a groomsman. All three weddings were wonderful.

How about children? You've seen those darling little ones, the flower girls and ring bearers who steal the show. They can be a wonderful addition to a wedding, yet they are by no means necessary. As for the cost of including children in your wedding party, they will add little to your budget except for the cost of the accessories they will carry or wear. The gifts you will give them can be inexpensive; costume jewelry or banks with change in them are appropriate. Lisa's wedding included six little flower girls and a boy who acted as ring bearer—all nieces, cousins, and a nephew of the bride and groom. They were wonderfully charming, and the added cost was negligible.

You almost certainly have people in mind whom you are considering as attendants. Fill in their names on the following chart, along with any thoughts concerning the wedding party that come to your mind—ideas for clothing, for instance, or for accessories, or gifts for the attendants.

Attendants ✤

Use this page as a worksheet while you think of the people you would like to ask to act as attendants. Space is also available for thoughts on clothing and accessories as well as for any other notes.

Bridesmaids   Phone

_____   _____

_____   _____

_____   _____

_____   _____

_____   _____

_____   _____

Junior Bridesmaids   Phone

_____   _____

_____   _____

Flower Girls   Phone

_____   _____

_____   _____

Dress styles I like:

_____

_____

Accessory ideas:

_____

Groomsmen   Phone

_____   _____

_____   _____

_____   _____

_____   _____

_____   _____

Ushers   Phone

_____   _____

_____   _____

_____   _____

Ring Bearers   Phone

_____   _____

_____   _____

Suit or Tuxedo styles I like:

_____

_____

Accessory ideas:

_____

_____

Notes:

_____

_____

THE GUEST LIST

Ready for your second rude awakening? It will likely come when you start making up the guest list. Before you know what's happening, that list can grow to unmanageable (and unaffordable) lengths.

When a couple is paying for their own wedding, the guest list is likely to be made up mostly of their mutual friends, with a sprinkling of close relatives from each family. When the bride's parents are paying, the guest list can turn into a real problem. It is only natural that Mom and Dad want to include more of their close friends and relatives, whom the bride hardly knows; and if they do, the groom's family will likely want to do the same.

But no matter who is paying for your wedding, it is certainly appropriate to limit your guest list to people who have known you and your husband-to-be, and who are truly interested in the two of you and your future together.

Here are two suggestions to help you keep the list under control:

- **Determine who it is you want at your wedding**. Family? Friends? People who are important to you and your fiancé's families? Business associates? Once you decide this, you will have a good focus point for assembling your guest list.

- **How many guests can you realistically and comfortably include?** Look at your budget, then at the capacity of your wedding site. Armed with this information, take your list of possible guests and chip away at it until it includes that number of people and no more. (Actually, you can invite a few more people than you can accommodate because there will undoubtedly be some who will not be able to attend. But be careful that you don't overestimate the number of declines.)

"That all sounds well and good," you might be saying, "but I don't know how I'll ever be able to limit my guest list. Everyone I see says they are looking forward to getting an invitation to my wedding. How can I get by without inviting everyone I've ever known—or who has ever known my family?"

Good question. Fortunately, there is a fairly simple answer: Tell the truth. Say you are having a small wedding—or that you are on a tight budget—and that you just aren't able to invite everyone you would like to have. Then thank the person for his or her interest in your wedding.

It will be harder to deal with your parents, and your soon-to-be parents-in-law, if they present you with impossibly long lists of potential guests. It's important to be gracious, and to be willing to compromise with them, but in the end, the final decision on the guest list is up to you and your fiancé—especially if you are paying the bills. It might help to meet with both families and discuss the matter together. Be honest about the financial constraints. Let everyone know that your budget simply will not allow you to stretch your guest list so far.

If you have been married before, it is absolutely appropriate to limit your ceremony guest list to your families and special friends. In fact, this is a common practice. And remember, you can follow a small wedding with a larger reception. On the other hand, you can have a large ceremony with a smaller, more intimate reception. The guest list does not have to be the same for both.

Should children be there? As you are planning your guest list, give some thought to whether you want to include children at the ceremony or the reception. Some people like to bring their children along to weddings, and it is true that it can be a great experience for those little folks. But it is also true that very young children can be disruptive. And kids do add to your limited guest list.

Should you include children? It's up to you. To let your guests know your wishes, put the names of the people you are inviting on the outside of the invitation. If you decide against the kids, spread the word that you will not be including children.

Uninvited guests. Even though you haven't encountered it yet, you are sure to be faced with a truly frustrating budget-buster: uninvited guests. As soon as your invitations are out you will certainly be presented with responses that cheerily state: "I know you'll enjoy meeting Jack. He'll be coming to your wedding with me." After all the planning you put into making up your guest list and keeping it under control, it isn't fair for you to have a lot of extra uninvited people to provide for. What to do? It is perfectly permissible for you to say to people who inform you that extra guests will be coming, "I'm sorry, but we simply cannot accommodate any more guests. Thank you for understanding."

Why all this emphasis on the guest list, you might ask? If you have plenty of room, what difference does it make who all comes? Well, maybe none at all. On the other hand, if the ceremony guest list translates over to the reception guest list, it can make a tremendous difference. Extra people will definitely mean higher costs for you—especially if families attending include dozens of cousins, nieces, and nephews.

We have included wedding guest worksheets (page 74) to guide you as you begin to put together your own guest list. If you will be having separate guest lists for the ceremony and the reception, you may want to make copies of the worksheet so you can fill in separate charts.

How are you doing so far? Managing to stay within your budget? If so, good for you! If not, go back to your master budget and see where you might do some adjusting.

Now, hold on to your hat and keep your master plan book clutched tightly in your hand. Starting with chapter 5, the budget going is likely to get rougher!

The Guest List ❧

Name and Address	Number Attending Wedding

Number Attending Reception	Gift Description	Date Thank-You Sent

The Guest List, continued

Name and Address	Number Attending Wedding

Number Attending Reception	Gift Description	Date Thank-You Sent

The Guest List, *continued*

Name and Address	Number Attending Wedding

Number Attending Reception	Gift Description	Date Thank-You Sent

The Guest List, continued

Name and Address	Number Attending Wedding

Number Attending Reception	Gift Description	Date Thank-You Sent

The Guest List, continued

Name and Address	Number Attending Wedding

Number Attending Reception	Gift Description	Date Thank-You Sent

The Guest List, continued

Name and Address	Number Attending Wedding

Number Attending Reception	Gift Description	Date Thank-You Sent

The Guest List, continued

Name and Address	Number Attending Wedding

Number Attending Reception	Gift Description	Date Thank-You Sent

The Guest List, *continued*

Name and Address	Number Attending Wedding

Number Attending Reception	Gift Description	Date Thank-You Sent

CHAPTER FIVE

The Early Bird Gets the Deal

Now it is time to get busy on all those decisions that need to be made early on: What kind of rings will you get and where will you get them? What will you wear? How about the rest of your wedding party? Where will you get your invitations? How about registering for gifts? There is a lot to do, so let's begin.

RINGS

When it comes to rings, **keep your budget firmly in mind, and be disciplined**. If you are just starting to shop, get ready for a real shock.

Actually, there is no need to feel pressured to buy an engagement ring right away. Many couples don't get one for years. It can be a wonderful gift on a special anniversary when money isn't quite so tight. And, yes, a special ring can be every bit as meaningful at a later date—maybe even more so!

Another possibility is having just one ring. You can combine the engagement ring and wedding ring in one wide band which may or may not be set with a stone.

If you do decide on an engagement ring, think *options.*

Most people think of engagement rings as diamond rings, but actually any stone is appropriate. Why not look at some other possibilities that will give you a unique ring with a lower price tag? Consider, for instance, this list of commonly used birthstones:

Birthstones

January	Garnet or Zircon
February	Amethyst
March	Aquamarine
April	Diamond
May	Emerald
June	Pearl
July	Ruby
August	Sardonyx or Peridot
September	Sapphire
October	Opal or Moonstone
November	Topaz
December	Turquoise or Lapis Lazuli

Nor must an engagement ring be new. Antique rings or family heirlooms can become engagement rings that are as meaningful as they are beautiful. Maxine proudly wore her grandmother's ruby ring. Sharon in New Mexico was given an engagement ring with a stunning turquoise, an heirloom from her groom-to-be's family reset just for her. Judy bought a secondhand ring for her husband-to-be and had it set with three small diamonds at a discount jewelry mart.

Don't be afraid to be imaginative!

BRIDAL APPAREL

Lisa had always intended that she would wear the wedding dress that her mother Kay had worn, a gown handmade by Kay's mother and grandmother. But shortly before Lisa was married, our home burned to the ground. We found ourselves unexpectedly going the rounds of bridal shops. What we found just about gave both of us heart attacks! According to the salesclerks, every dress looked "fabulous" on Lisa, and every one of them was just "made" for her. In the end, because we didn't know we had alternatives, we paid over $1,000 for a gown at a bridal shop.

Without a doubt, bridal shops are the most expensive way to get a wedding gown. Prices range from an average of $900 in the Northeast to $500 in the Midwest. And this doesn't include the extras, such as a headpiece and veil (they run between $100 and $200), shoes ($50), a petticoat ($50), and various undergarments.

If you decide to go the bridal shop route, remember that it is *your* dress and *your* wedding and *your* choice. Refuse to be flattered, intimidated, or pushed into making a quick decision. Have your budgeted amount firmly in mind when you walk into a shop, and don't let a salesperson talk you into spending more. If you are feeling confused, uncertain, or pressured, say, "Thank you. I'll think about it. May I have your card so I can get back in touch with you?"

Many bridal shops have sales that offer their samples at great prices. One charming shop on the Oregon coast carried designer gowns priced from $795 to $1,595; samples of the same gowns were on sale for $99 to $399. A shop in central California has an annual January sale where gowns normally priced from $500 to $1,500 are sold for $100. "Last year we sold thirty wedding dresses in thirty-five minutes!" the shop owner told us.

Call the shops in your area and ask if there is a particular time of year that they have such sales. (We found them most common in the fall.) You should also be aware that samples usually come in size ten. If that isn't your size, you may be able to have alterations made. But don't buy a gown figuring, "I'll diet and lose enough weight to go down two sizes before the wedding." You will likely end up squashed into a too-small gown at best, or at worst buying a new one at the last minute because you can't squeeze into that "super deal."

No appropriate samples available? Here are some other possibilities for affordable bridal wear.

Choose a formal. It used to be that brides were blushing young women fresh out of high school or college. Not any more. The typical bride of today is older and has been living on her own, busily building a career. Almost one third of all brides have been married before. The fashion industry has responded to these changes by introducing more informal wedding gowns—pastel or off-white, anywhere from street-to ankle length, no train.

Prom and bridesmaid dresses are often available for under $100. They may need some alterations to make them appropriate for a bride to wear, however. For instance, puffed sleeves can be added to strapless gowns, trains can be made of a matching fabric or of lace. Can't sew, you say? A friend with a sewing machine and a bit of know-how might be able to do the job for you. If not, a professional seamstress would likely do the job for a reasonable price. (We were quoted hourly rates all the way from $6 to $20 an hour. Be sure and ask the total cost *before* agreeing to the job!)

Check department stores. Some department stores have excellent selections of bridal attire at a fraction of what you would pay at a bridal salon. JCPenney is a good example. There are over forty JCPenney stores in nineteen states that have actual bridal salons where you can see lovely gowns priced as low as $300.

If you don't happen to live near one of these stores—or even if you do—you may want to check the JCPenney Bridal Collection mail-order catalog. It is well-done and offers a number of attractive bridal dresses as inexpensive as $130 and formal wedding gowns for as little $220. They also offer a full selection of accessories, as well as bridesmaids dresses. And it takes less than a week to get your new dress! To receive a copy of the catalog, call toll free 1-800-527-8345.

Buy discount. Many larger cities have factory outlet stores that sell evening wear and prom dresses that can work quite well as bridal dresses. And they offer prices up to 80 percent off the regular retail prices! One of our favorites is the Gunne Sax outlet in San Francisco, which has an entire room dedicated to wedding attire.

One warning: Outlet shopping can be time-consuming. Allow yourself plenty of time to search through the racks for something suitable in your size. And be prepared for the possibility that you will not find what you want. Sometimes the selection is incredible, but at other times it is disappointing. On the other hand, searching through the racks and finding a beautiful designer dress for $100 can be a great investment of your time.

To find an outlet store in your area, check the Yellow Pages under "Bridal."

The Discount Bridal Service (DBS) is another possibility. With over three hundred representatives nationwide, DBS offers discounts of up to 40 percent on just about all nationally advertised bridal wear. (That's right! They carry those same dresses you see in the bridal magazines at sky-high prices!) Headquartered in Silver Spring, Maryland, they have representatives in most major cities and in parts of Canada. Find the gown you like in a bridal shop, then tell your local DBS representative the manufacturer and style (or if you saw the gown in a bride's magazine, give the issue and page number). The representative will give you a price quote and take it from there. To insure that you order the right size, DBS will make available to you a manufacturer's size chart which you can compare with your own measurements. Their delivery time is fourteen to sixteen weeks. "We won't take an order if there isn't time to fill it," a representative at their headquarters states. "We have been in business twelve years, and have never missed a wedding."

Many DBS representatives also offer discounts on wedding invitations and other accessories. To locate the DBS representative nearest you, call toll free 1-800-874-8794.

One more idea: If you like the delicate European look, you may want to check one of the Laura Ashley stores. Although it isn't a discount store, Laura Ashley carries lovely bridal wear with price tags of approximately $300 to $600. These stores are located in thirty-nine locations throughout the United States and Canada. To locate the store nearest you, call 1-800-367-2000.

Use a free seamstress. Are you experienced at sewing? Do you have a talented mother or cousin or grandmother who is? If you have access to a free seamstress, you can buy one of the many attractive patterns available in fabric stores, as well as fabric and trim, and have a lovely gown for approximately $150 (depending on the pattern, fabric, and trim you choose).

There are many advantages to having a custom-made gown. For one thing, you can have just the gown you want in exactly the right fabric, and trimmed especially for you. Another advantage is that it can be made to fit you perfectly (an important consideration if you don't happen to be a classic size). And it will cost just a fraction of what you would pay for a store-bought dress.

But there are also some warnings. A wedding gown is no project for a beginner. Be sure the person doing the sewing knows what she is doing. Our suggestion is to get the pattern, then make up the dress bodice and sleeves out of an old sheet. Don't worry about doing it neatly and carefully. All you want is an idea of how you will look in the style and how it will fit you. Disappointed with the sheet dress? Then put the pattern in a drawer and invest another $6 or so in a different pattern, get another old sheet from a thrift store, and start again.

When your sheet dress fits you well, and you are satisfied that it is as flattering as a dress made out of an old sheet can be, you will be ready to lay the pattern out on the real fabric and start cutting.

Fabric store employees will be happy to help you find everything you need. But it's a good idea to wait to buy your fabric until you are happy with your sheet dress. Otherwise you may not have the right amount for the dress pattern you finally decide on.

Hire a seamstress. Of course, many brides will not have access to a competent free seamstress. Another option is to hire a seamstress. She will likely be willing to help you shop for the pattern and fabric. Many of the same advantages we talked about for a free seamstress hold true with a hired seamstress: The dress can be made just the way you want it, and it will fit you perfectly. Another advantage of hiring someone is that at this stressful time, it will be one less thing for you to worry about.

Hiring a seamstress can cost less than purchasing a gown, although when we checked we found that the cost is often the same. One seamstress who has made a number of bridal gowns told us, "When people come to me wanting a budget wedding gown, or wanting a gown in a hurry, I tell them they would do better to buy off the rack." Her price is not cheap, she says, and her lead time is a minimum of six months. A good round-figure price for a basic wedding gown is $200-$300. As you add lace and beading, the price quickly increases. An intricately decorated dress can carry a price tag of $1,500 to $2,000.

One seamstress had this word of advice: "Before you bring a seamstress a picture of your dream dress, try on a similar one. It's heartbreaking to get a dress made and then discover that it doesn't look nearly as good on you as it did on the six-foot, one-hundred-ten pound model in the magazine!"

Borrow a dress. Many of your friends and relatives are likely to have wedding gowns hanging in the back of their closets. Most would be happy and flattered if you asked to wear their gowns. It would be easiest if the borrowed gown was your size. But if it isn't, it's possible to have it altered. Of course, this would mean you would be responsible for having it altered back to its original size. Be sure to record the exact amount a seam is taken in or let out.

You may also need to have the dress dry-cleaned before it is worn (this will cost approximately $75). If it is an old dress (your mother's, for instance) it may have discolorations or spots that will have to be removed. But even with the extra charges for alterations and cleaning, your costs will be low.

Judy wore her mother's wedding dress and was able to do the alterations herself. Because it was a plainer dress than Judy had in mind, she added French lace and beading. To get the flared effect she wanted around the hemline, she decided to use fishing line. When she saw she would have to buy a whole roll of line at a cost of $10, she persuaded a local sporting goods store clerk to give her some old line which she untangled and bleached. "It worked fine!" Judy said. Her perfectly fitting, custom-made, newly dry-cleaned dress cost her just $150.

Rent a dress. Many beautiful and expensive dresses are available for rental. If the fit isn't right, they can usually be altered. Although the costs vary widely from shop to shop across the country and Canada, even very expensive dresses can generally be rented for under $250, and many are far less costly. A rental shop in Honolulu, for instance, advertises rental dresses between $90 and $200. One in Philadelphia advertises $2,000 designer dresses at rental prices of $250.

Most larger cities have wedding gowns for rent, and many smaller cities do as well. Check for rental stores in the yellow pages under "Bridal Attire," "Costumes," "Wedding Rentals," and "Rentals."

Check newspaper ads. Now, don't be so quick to turn up your nose. You may be surprised at what you can find advertised in the newspaper. It's a sad fact that some wedding dresses are purchased and never worn, and many owners are ready to sell the dresses at a sacrifice. We found an ad that read: "New wedding dress, never worn, size fourteen. Originally $750, will sacrifice at $200." Another read: "Designer wedding gown, size ten. Originally $1,800. Asking $400 OBO." Still another simply stated: "New wedding dress, $100."

Are these good bargains? Are they gowns you would like? The only way to find out is to call the number listed and ask questions. If you are impressed with what you hear, go to see the gown and try it on. If you are pleased with the way it looks and fits, make a low offer (you can always come up). Most owners are anxious to sell.

Look through antique clothing shops. You never know, you just might find the right dress at an antique store. General antique stores often display Victorian-style dresses for sale along with brass beds or mahogany hope chests. Vintage clothing stores also can have unexpected finds at great prices.

And don't rule out thrift stores and flea markets. One woman found a lovely ivory prom dress that was still wrapped in its original plastic. The price tag read $30. Another found an antique lace dress similar to one she had seen elsewhere for $625. She bought the dress for $20!

One bride told us, "With three children and almost nothing to spend on my wedding, I had just about given up on having a wedding dress at all. Then I found one in a Salvation Army thrift store. It's beautiful and a perfect fit. I couldn't be happier!"

The lessons here? **Check everywhere, and stay open-minded.** There are great bargains out there. All you have to do is find them.

What is the *right* wedding dress? Whatever makes you feel beautiful and comfortable and happy. Whether your wedding dress is long or short, fancy or simple, old or new, choose the one that's uniquely you and fits your budget, and you will have the perfect dress for your wedding.

Other bridal apparel. If you were shocked at the price of wedding gowns, just wait until you see the price tags on the finishing touches to bridal costumes. In bridal shops, headpieces and veils average between $250 and $400. That is really frustrating when you think of what you're getting for your money—a $10 headpiece and another $10 of veil fabric. Quite a markup, isn't it?

Unlike wedding gowns, veils are simple to make. Everything you need—headpieces, veiling, and lace—is available in most fabric stores. Depending on what you want, you can probably make a veil for $20 to $30. If making it yourself doesn't seem workable to you, look into renting. We checked one rental shop that had a whole wall of headpieces and veils that ranged between $25 and $35.

The main thing to remember about your headpiece is that it should coordinate with your dress. For example, don't use different styles of lace on your dress and your veil. The length of your veil should be determined by the length of your gown: a street-length dress is complimented by a shorter veil, while a floor-length gown calls for a veil of fingertip length. If your wedding is to be informal, you may decide to skip the veil and wear a hat, or perhaps a flower or bow in your hair.

We cannot think of a single good reason to buy shoes, slips, or undergarments in a bridal shop. All these are available much more inexpensively in department stores, including Sears and JCPenney, and through JCPenney's catalog.

You can likely borrow or rent a wedding slip (which could easily cost you $100 to buy) even more easily than a gown. Closets everywhere contain these "wear-once-and-what-to-do-with-them-now?" garments.

There is no reason to invest in quality shoes. In a bridal shop they can run over $100 a pair, yet similar looking shoes can easily be found at regular stores—including discount clothing places such as Wal-Mart or Ross Department Stores, or a discount shoe store for as little as $20. If your gown is long, you might even want to consider a slipper-type whoe in a white fabric. With flat or low heels and round toes, they are extremely comfortable—and inexpensive.

The following chart will help you decide upon and price your bridal outfit.

Bridal Wear ✤

Dress

OPTION 1   Cost: $ _____ Size: _____

Description: _____

_____

_____

_____

Contact Person: _____

Phone: _____

OPTION 2   Cost: $ _____ Size: _____

Description: _____

_____

_____

_____

Contact Person: _____

Phone: _____

OPTION 3   Cost: $ _____ Size: _____

Description: _____

_____

_____

_____

Contact Person: _____

Phone: _____

Accessories

	Description:	Cost:
Hosiery		
Lingerie		
Jewelry		
Shoes		

Headpiece and Veil

OPTION 1 Cost: $ _____

Description: _____

_____

_____

OPTION 2 Cost: $ _____

Description: _____

_____

_____

OPTION 3 Cost: $ _____

Description: _____

_____

_____

Do you want to wear a garter that your new husband can throw at the reception? It is easy to make. Here are the instructions:

Make Your Own Garter

If you've seen expensive garters for sale in bridal stores, you'll be surprised how affordable and easy they are to make.

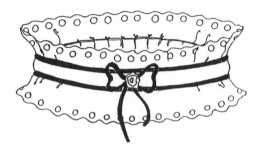

1. Start with a piece of elastic one inch wide. You can find this at any fabric store.

2. Measure the elastic so that it fits comfortably but snugly, just above or just below your knee.

3. On a sewing machine or by hand, make a fabric tube that is as long as the elastic is when it is stretched to its full length.

4. Sew some pretty lace onto the tube.

5. Slide the elastic into the tube and stitch the ends together.

6. Find any decorations that you like, such as ribbons, bows, flowers, or pearls and sew them on.

7. Now you have a beautiful garter that you can proudly say you made yourself.

WHAT WILL THE REST OF THE
BRIDAL PARTY WEAR?

Even though your bridesmaids will pay for their own outfits, it will be up to you to decide what they will wear. And your attendants will surely appreciate you keeping cost in mind when you choose for them. But cost isn't the only important consideration. Think, too, of how the dresses you are considering will look on each of the bridesmaids, not only in relation to style and color, but also keeping age and body type in mind. A dress that is charmingly elegant on a tall, thin twenty-year-old can make a short thirty-five-year-old look mighty silly.

Since a bridesmaid dress can be a substantial investment, it is considerate to select a style that your attendants may be able to wear after the wedding. If your bridesmaids can sew, or if they have friends or relatives who can, you might want to consider choosing fabric and a pattern they can sew, which can be much more reasonable than buying a dress. Judy and her six bridesmaids got together with a few other volunteer seamstresses and made the bridesmaids' dresses on one marathon workday. It was fun and the work was done quickly.

For a small, informal wedding, you may decide to have your bridesmaid wear an outfit she already owns. This is often done in second marriages when the bride has just one attendant.

You should have some idea of the cost of the outfit when you choose your wedding party so that you can let your friends know what is expected of them *before* they make a commitment. Some of your friends simply may not be able to afford it. We know of one young lady who has seven bridesmaid's dresses hanging in her closet. "I'm really pleased that so many of my friends have honored me," she says. "But I simply cannot afford to be in one more wedding!"

Hint: You may be able to help out by giving your attendants gifts of accessories you want them to wear

Attendant Attire ❧

	Outfit Description	Size
Honor Attendant:		
Bridesmaid:		
Bridesmaid:		
Bridesmaid:		
Bridesmaid:		
Bridesmaid:		
Bridesmaid:		
Flower Girl:		

Fitting Dates:

Cost / Source	Shoes/Accessories	
$	Item:	Cost:
$	Item:	Cost:
$	Item:	Cost:
$	Item:	Cost:
$	Item:	Cost:
$	Item:	Cost:
$	Item:	Cost:
$	Item:	Cost:

Notes:

Attendant Attire, continued

	Outfit Description	Size
Groom:		
Best Man:		
Groomsman:		
Groomsman:		
Groomsman:		
Groomsman:		
Groomsman:		
Groomsman:		
Ring Bearer:		

Fitting Dates:

Cost / Source	Shoes/Accessories	
$	Item:	Cost:
$	Item:	Cost:
$	Item:	Cost:
$	Item:	Cost:
$	Item:	Cost:
$	Item:	Cost:
$	Item:	Cost:
$	Item:	Cost:
$	Item:	Cost:

Notes:

during the ceremony. Necklaces, gloves, or shoes are good choices. One bride whose attendants would be making their own dresses made them a gift of the fabric.

The best approach to purchasing bridesmaid dresses is to have each attendant pay for her dress when it is ordered, or when she picks it up. Maureen learned this lesson the hard way. "I picked out the dresses for my four attendants and, to make it easier, put the entire amount—over $400!—on my credit card with the understanding that they would pay me back as soon as possible. Well, almost a year has gone by and not a one has paid me back! I felt so bad about asking them for the money that I put it off for a long time. Finally I wrote to each one, then when I got no answer, I called. But all I got were stories about how tight things were for them. So in the end, a big chunk of my budget went to dresses that are hanging in their closets!"

As Maureen can attest, once the wedding is over it can be next to impossible to collect debts.

Traditionally, groomsmen wear rented tuxedoes which they pay for themselves. Today, however, more and more couples are electing to have their groomsmen wear dark suits, which many of the men already own. The ones who don't can rent them relatively reasonably. In small, informal weddings, some couples are even dispensing with the suits altogether. Amy's wedding at the botanical garden featured bridesmaids in floral print cotton dresses and groomsmen in slacks, white shirts, and bow ties. For her beach wedding, Angela's attendants wore gauzy summer dresses and the groomsmen wore slacks and open neck shirts.

The flower girl's dress should be appropriate for her age, and should harmonize with the bridesmaids' gowns in color and fabric. She may carry a new basket, or you can spruce up a white or wicker Easter basket. The ring bearer may wear any color suit or dressy outfit, usually dark in the winter and light in the summer. He will need a clean, satin pillow for the rings. (For more on the ring bearer's pillow, see chapter 7.)

INVITATIONS, THANK-YOU NOTES, AND OTHER STATIONERY

The average couple spends $350 to $400 for invitations and other wedding stationery, such as response cards and thank-you notes. Prices vary from store to store, so here is another area in which it really pays to shop around.

Invitations. You can get the cost down to $.35 to $.40 per invitation—including both inner and outer envelope, and an RSVP card and envelope—if you order them from a paper supply store. The invitations will come blank, so you will have to take them to a quick-print shop and have them printed, a process that will generally cost less than $20 for a set of one hundred. If you bring along a good quality copy of your wording exactly as you want it to appear—either printed out on a laser printer or prepared by a calligrapher—you won't have to pay a typesetting fee.

A number of companies offer a variety of attractive yet inexpensive wedding invitations by mail order. Most have toll-free numbers, and will send free catalogs and samples upon request. To get the names and telephone numbers, check the advertisements in recent issues of bridal magazines. One warning here: If you decide to order printed invitations by mail, make certain that if there is a mistake in the printing, your order will be fixed at no cost.

You can get some good buys from manufacturers, too. One we especially recommend is Regency, which has some of the best buys around. Although there is an enormous variety of styles (and prices!) displayed in their sample books, they start as low as $38.90 for quantities of one hundred. (This price includes the invitation, double envelopes, and tissues. One design has a gold-lined envelope, another a floral print liner.) Since Regency has such a large distribution among stationery shops and printing companies, you can find their sample books almost anywhere. "If you are on a tight budget," one stationer advises, "limit yourself to the first couple of pages of the sample book. They get more expensive with each page you turn." If you order from Regency, you can expect to get your invitations within a week. (For more information, you can contact Regency toll free at 1-800-831-5057.)

An excellent way to save even more on your invitations is to go the "no extras" route. If you have "reception following" printed at the bottom of the invitations, you won't have to buy reception cards. That alone can save you approximately 15 percent (and that's not counting the 50 percent you will save on the cost of postage). You can also skip the envelope linings, and omit the response cards unless you need to have an accurate count for the reception. Any salesperson showing you invitations will try to convince you that you also need engraved napkins and matchbooks, engraved programs, and a variety of other products you can almost certainly do without. This is a good time to practice your sales resistance!

If you are planning to have your return address printed on the envelopes, why not consider buying an embosser with your return address instead? Many mail-order catalogs offer them for less than $10.

However you make your order, add an extra twenty-five or so invitations and envelopes. This is good insurance. If you have to go back and order more later for those really important people who somehow slipped your mind, they will be a whole lot more expensive.

If you are planning a small, informal wedding, it is better—and less expensive—to send personal notes, either in your parents' names or in yours. (More older couples, and those who have been married before, are leaving the names of the parents off the invitation altogether.) Your short note, written in black ink on plain ivory or white paper, might say something such as:

Dear Anne and Joseph,

I will be married to Bill Macy in my home on Saturday, July 25, at 1:00 p.m. A reception will follow in the garden. We would love to have you join us.

Affectionately,
Julia

Thank-you notes. When you are ordering invitations, don't forget the thank-you notes. You will be needing them soon. Traditional thank-you notes are plain white or off-white. While they can be engraved with your names or initials, this is by no means necessary. You can buy your notes in bulk from a paper supply house at great savings.

You will cut your postage costs nearly in half if you are careful to choose invitations that are *not* oversized. And speaking of postage, a nice way to give a personal touch at no extra cost is to check with your post office for stamps that are especially wedding friendly. Lisa used stamps with a red heart made of roses and the word "love" on them. How thoughtful of the U.S. Postal Service to provide them! Commemorative stamps are also available with birds or flowers. It's worth checking to see what the post office has available.

Even though you are working hard to stay within your budget, there are some places you definitely should *not* cut corners. These include asking your guests to pay for their own reception dinner, asking them to contribute money to you in lieu of a wedding gift, and making requests for money on your wedding invitations. It is your party, and you must give it at your expense, no strings attached. Smaller and less expensive is fine. Billing your guests absolutely is not.

Stationery Estimate &

Invitations

OPTION 1 Company: _____

Address: _____

Contact Person: _____

Phone: _____

Book:_____ Style No. _____

Qty.:_____ Cost:_____

Deposit: _____

OPTION 2 Company: _____

Address: _____

Contact Person: _____

Phone: _____

Book: _____ Style No. _____

Qty.: _____ Cost: _____

Deposit: _____

OPTION 3 Company: _____

Address: _____

Contact Person: _____

Phone: _____

Book:_____ Style No. _____

Qty.:_____ Cost:_____

Deposit: _____

Thank-You Notes

OPTION 1 Company: _____

Address: _____

Contact Person: _____

Phone: _____

Book:_____ Style No. _____

Qty.:_____ Cost: _____

Deposit: _____

OPTION 2 Company: _____

Address: _____

Contact Person: _____

Phone: _____

Book:_____ Style No. _____

Qty.:_____ Cost: _____

Deposit: _____

OPTION 3 Company: _____

Address: _____

Contact Person: _____

Phone: _____

Book:_____ Style No. _____

Qty.:_____ Cost: _____

Deposit: _____

Stationery Estimate, continued

Other _____

OPTION 1   Company: _____

Address: _____

Contact Person: _____

Phone: _____

Book: _____   Style No. _____

Qty.: _____   Cost: _____

Deposit: _____

OPTION 2   Company: _____

Address: _____

Contact Person: _____

Phone: _____

Book: _____   Style No. _____

Qty.: _____   Cost: _____

Deposit: _____

OPTION 3   Company: _____

Address: _____

Contact Person: _____

Phone: _____

Book: _____   Style No. _____

Qty.: _____   Cost: _____

Deposit: _____

REGISTERING FOR GIFTS

You probably know all about registering for wedding gifts. This free service is provided by department stores and gift shops, no strings attached. It is well worth your time to look around several places and register for the gifts you would like to receive at each. If you don't register, you will find that instead of the pans, sheets, towels, Chinese style flower vase, and floral print tablecloth you want, you will get seven crystal picture frames, ten large salad bowls, an orange flower vase, and a plaid tablecloth in all the wrong colors. Even if you register you are sure to receive some impractical, duplicate (and even downright ugly) gifts, but you will come much closer to getting what you need and want. Together you and your husband-to-be can choose the colors and designs and products that fit your taste, decor, and needs. If you let your guests know what china patterns, glassware, flatware, linens, and so forth you have selected, it will cut down enormously on the time it would otherwise take you to return and exchange the gifts your well-intentioned guests spent so much time selecting for you.

When you are deciding where to register, don't overlook such places as Pier 1 Imports and Strouds for discount kitchen, bedroom, and bath supplies. (Strouds is not nationwide. Call 1-800-STROUDS to see if there is a store near you.) Also look for discount stores unique to your area, such as Design Linens in Oregon.

When it's not the first time. "But," you may be saying, "we have both been married before. Each of us set up house-keeping long ago. In fact, we have doubles of almost everything. What should we do about wedding gifts?"

The answer is simple: register just as if you were a young, first time bride. In fact, for couples like you, or for singles who have already set up their homes, registering is especially important. Knowing your situation, your guests will be so perplexed about what to give you that you can count on the "unusual" (read that "odd") gift. Surely there are some things you need. Are your towels wearing thin, your pillowcases mismatched, or your sheets faded? Do you have three glasses with your old initial, four with pictures of antique cars, and eight others of assorted sizes and styles? How about the kitchen spice racks and utensil organizers that are all the rage? Or the book you would love to have for your coffee table?

Judy and Jason registered at the Home Improvement Center and asked for a garden hose, a rake, and a doorbell (all of which they received, by the way).

"But," you may insist, "what we really need is money!" We know how you feel, but your financial situation is not the problem of your guests. If they give money, great—and some probably will. But *don't ask for it!* The whole idea of wedding gifts is to help the new couple set up housekeeping, not to help them make the rent or pay off bills.

It may be that you would prefer not to receive wedding gifts at all, especially if you already have your home set up. One woman suggested making donations to a specified charity in lieu of sending a gift. What a generous idea!

To help you decide which items you might want to put on your gift registry list, we have prepared a basic inventory sheet. Use it as a starting point, then move on to your own specific ideas and desires. Be sure to include some inexpensive items as well as a few expensive ones that several families can go in on together.

Gift Registry Checklist ❖

Along with your dream gifts, be sure to include some inexpensive items. Many of the people who would like to buy gifts for you cannot afford an entire place setting of china, silver, or crystal.

Qty.	Price	Formal Dinnerware		Store
		Brand	Pattern	
		Dinner Plates		
		Salad/Dessert Plates		
		Cups/Saucers		
		Soup Bowls		
		Serving Bowls		
		Platter		
		Vegetable Bowls		
		Gravy Boat		

Qty.	Price	Glassware		Store
		Brand	Pattern	
		Water Goblets		
		Wine Glasses		
		Tumblers		
		Juice Glasses		

Qty.	Price	Casual Dinnerware		Store
		Brand	Pattern	
		Dinner Plates		
		Salad/Dessert Plates		
		Soup/Cereal Bowls		
		Cups/Saucers		
		Bread Plates		
		Sugar Bowl/Creamer		

Gift Registry Checklist, *continued*

Qty.	Price	Casual Dinnerware, continued	Store
		Casseroles	
		Serving Platter	
		Butter Dish	
		Mugs	
		Gravy Boat	
		Cannisters	

Qty.	Price	Silverware		Store
		Brand	Pattern	
		Knives		
		Forks		
		Salad Forks		
		Soup Spoons		
		Teaspoons		
		Butter Knife		
		Serving Spoons/Forks		
		Gravy Ladle		
		Sugar Spoon		
		Silver Chest		

Qty.	Price	Flatware		Store
		Brand	Pattern	
		Knives		
		Forks		
		Salad Forks		
		Teaspoons		
		Soup Spoons		
		Serving Spoons/Forks		
		Gravy Ladle		
		Utensils		

Qty.	Price	Serving Pieces		Store
		Brand	Pattern	
		Teapot		
		Serving Trays		
		Hot Plate		
		Cake Plate		
		Salad Set		
		Salt/Pepper Shakers		
		Pepper Mill		
		Soup Tureen		

Qty.	Price	Kitchen Appliances	Color/ Pattern	Store
		Toaster		
		Coffee Maker		
		Coffee Grinder		
		Microwave Oven		
		Waffle Maker		
		Juicer		
		Blender		
		Mixer		
		Crock Pot		
		Food Processor		
		Can Opener		
		Iron		

Qty.	Price	Kitchen Linens	Color/ Pattern	Store
		Dish Towels		
		Dish Cloths		
		Pot Holders		
		Aprons		

Gift Registry Checklist, continued

Qty.	Price	Table Linens	Color/Pattern	Store
		Tablecloth		
		Table Runner		
		Napkins		
		Place Mats		
		Napkin Rings		

Qty.	Price	Home Decorations	Color/Pattern	Store
		Lamps		
		Clocks		
		Picture Frames		
		Mirrors		
		Vases		
		Candlesticks		
		Curtains/Blinds		

Qty.	Price	Bedroom Linens	Size	Color/Pattern	Store
		Flat Sheets			
		Fitted Sheets			
		Pillows			
		Pillow Cases			
		Mattress Pad			
		Blankets			
		Comforter/Bedspread			

Qty.	Price	Bath Linens/Accessories	Color/Pattern	Store
		Bath Towels		
		Hand Towels		
		Washcloths		

Qty.	Price	Bath Accessories, continued	Color/ Pattern	Store
		Guest Towels		
		Bath Mat		
		Soap Dish		
		Cup		
		Toothbrush Holder		
		Scale		

Qty.	Price	Home Electronics	Description	Store
		Television		
		Clock Radio		
		Wall Clock		
		Stereo Components		
		Cassette Player		
		CD Player		
		VCR		
		Camera		
		Telephone		
		Answering Machine		

Qty.	Price	Other	Store

As each gift arrives, be sure to record it on your guest list worksheet. You may feel certain that you will never forget it was Mavis at the office who gave you the duck pillows, but we know from experience that even the most memorable gifts can slip your mind. Then, as you write your thank-you note, check the gift off on your worksheet. (The empty blanks will nag you into keeping up to date on those thank-yous!)

YOUR BEST FACE FORWARD

One last early-on suggestion: You will want to look your very best on your wedding day. If you are thinking of a new hairdo or a different makeup approach, now is a good time to start experimenting. If you like the look, hang on to it. If not, you have plenty of time to start over.

You have finished a lot of your preparation. Feels good, doesn't it? Now, with this solid foundation laid, you are ready to make some exciting decisions about the music, the photography, and the flowers.

CHAPTER SIX

Music, Flowers, and Pictures

"**M**y roommate has a really nice voice. Maybe she could sing at my wedding. And her husband plays guitar. If they did all the music, it would save me a bundle."

"Florists are so expensive! Couldn't I just get some flowers and do without the professional?"

"Just about everyone I know has a camera. If they all take pictures at my wedding and reception, I should get enough good prints to fill an album. And my brother could make a video."

Musicians? Florist? Photographer? Videographer? Do you really have to hire all those professionals in order to have music and flowers at your wedding, and pictures to enjoy afterward? Maybe. Then again, maybe not. Let's look at some of the cost-saving options you have in these important—and potentially budget-busting—areas.

MUSIC

Your ceremony music may be as simple as a church organ, or as elaborate as a string ensemble and a group of vocalists. For your reception, the choices are broader still—from nothing at all, all the way up to a live band. Although the costs can vary widely depending on what and who you want and where you live, the average amount spent on entertainment for a wedding ceremony and reception combined is $1,000.

Is that you crying, "Yikes!"? Let us quickly assure you that *you do not have to spend this much.* There are a number of cost-cutting possibilities, first for your ceremony, then for your reception.

Ceremony music. We'll begin with the least expensive options, and there is no better place to start than free music.

Free Music. Musically gifted relatives and friends can do wonders for your ceremony budget. There is probably talent all around you, though it might be hiding in unexpected places. Perhaps your niece is first chair violinist in the high school orchestra, or it may be that your groom's cousin is an accomplished vocalist. Of course, it may be that your niece is the *only* violinist in her high school, or that the cousin's mother's idea of "accomplished" is vastly different from yours. Since the music will go a long way toward setting the mood for your ceremony, you don't want a shaky or squawky amateur performance. So it makes sense to check the performer out before you make a commitment to a friend or relative. It is also a good idea to get an honest opinion from other people who have heard the person perform in public.

Volunteer musicians don't need to be the usual keyboard or vocalist folks. Think toward unique and unexpected possibilities. For instance, Patricia and her fiancé worked with a children's church group for several years. To the delight of their wedding guests, their ceremony music was provided by the twenty-six earnest voices of the six-, seven-, and eight-year-olds in the primary choir.

Professional and amateur combination. As an alternative to all-amateur music, you might consider hiring one professional, then rounding the ceremony out with the volunteer talent of friends or relatives. Since a good organist or pianist can be hard to find, hiring one may be the best use of your ceremony budget. On the other hand, you may have a friend who is an accomplished organist or pianist, and what you need is a good soloist. Or you may not want an organist at all. You can decide where the money is best spent.

Music fresh and canned. Tammy borrowed classical CDs from her friends and put together a tape of beautiful music for her wedding. She paced it out carefully, recording just the number of minutes appropriate for each period of the ceremony. She also recorded an accompaniment for a friend who sang a beautiful version of Paul Stookey's "Wedding Song."

If you decide to pre-record a cassette tape with music you select, carefully organize it to coordinate with the order of your ceremony, beginning with the seating of the guests and ending with the recessional. Each section should be timed so that the recording will neither stop abruptly, nor will it end too soon. (Someone should be prepared to operate it manually in case something unexpected happens, however.) If your friends don't have the selections you want, check your public library or a school's music library. You may need to invest in a new copy of a particular album to assure that you get just what you want both in the type of music and the quality of the recording..

When you record your tape, use good quality, high fidelity recording equipment. If your own system isn't quite up to the task, find a music-lover friend who will make the recording for you on state-of-the-art equipment.

You will need someone to start and stop the tape at the appropriate times. If your site has a sound system, have your volunteer—and perhaps a backup person as well—get careful instructions on how to play your tape through it. If there is no sound system, or if you are being married at home or in an outdoor setting, you may have to rent sound equipment.

Untapped local talent. Nonprofessional musicians of all sorts—both instrumentalists and vocalists—are available locally, and many have quite a bit of experience performing at weddings. For references, call music directors at churches in your area, or ask other brides for suggestions. Good sources of untapped talent are music schools and the music departments at local colleges and universities where many students pick up extra money by performing.

As you think through these options, jot down your thoughts and ideas on the Ceremony Music Options chart. Then use the next chart to record your final ceremony music plan.

Reception music. You may decide not to have music at your reception. If you do want music, here are some options for you to consider. (Again, remember that the costs quoted are approximate.)

Volunteer or amateur musicians. Because a reception setting is often less formal than the marriage ceremony, your reception can lend itself especially well to the volunteer talents of your friends and relatives. All kinds of music are appropriate at receptions. Guitarist? Fine. Jazz pianist? Wonderful. Accordion player? Sure. Chamber quartet? Super. Ethnic musicians? Great. Whatever you want is just right.

Your reception can be filled with fabulously entertaining music. All you have to do is find the musicians, and they are everywhere. A nurse we know has recently been unmasked as a club singer, and a good one at that. The husband of Lisa's third grade teacher is in a string quartet that looks for any

Ceremony Music Options ✤

OPTION 1 Music Plan: _____

__ Volunteer Musicians   __ Other Musicians   __ Pre-recorded Music

Contact Person: _____ Phone: _____

Equipment Needed: _____

Helpers Needed: _____

Notes: _____

_____

Cost: $ _____ Choice: __ Yes   __ No

OPTION 2 Music Plan: _____

__ Volunteer Musicians   __ Other Musicians   __ Pre-recorded Music

Contact Person: _____ Phone: _____

Equipment Needed: _____

Helpers Needed: _____

Notes: _____

_____

Cost: $ _____ Choice: __ Yes   __ No

OPTION 3 Music Plan: _____

__ Volunteer Musicians   __ Other Musicians   __ Pre-recorded Music

Contact Person: _____ Phone: _____

Equipment Needed: _____

Helpers Needed: _____

Notes: _____

_____

Cost: $ _____ Choice: __ Yes   __ No

Ceremony Music Plan ⚘

	Phone	Cost
Instrumentalists		
Vocalists		
	Total Cost	$
	Deposit Paid	$
	Balance Due	$

Music Selections

Prelude: _____

_____

Processional: _____

_____

During Ceremony: _____

_____

Recessional: _____

_____

Postlude: _____

opportunity to perform together. A machinist in our church is a trained operatic baritone. Everywhere there are engineers, secretaries, stockbrokers, plumbers, mail carriers, and all sorts of other people who just happen to be musically talented. Keep your eyes and ears open, and let your friends and relatives know you are looking.

Note: Unless the musician is a friend or relative, you should expect (and offer) to pay an honorarium.

Piped-in music. You can get free music over the sound system. Many halls and restaurants have background music already programmed and ready for you to use. When you reserve your reception site, ask what music might be available. But before you sign on the dotted line, be sure to listen to what they have to offer. If it isn't your kind of music, it's no bargain even if it is free.

Disk jockey. If you like the band sound, think about a disk jockey. It's a whole lot cheaper than hiring a band! You can hire a professional DJ (which may cost you more than you want to spend) or you can look for an amateur, which may run about $50.

Believe it or not, there are young people who own their own DJ equipment and are looking for opportunities to use it in public and pick up a few dollars. The problem is, not all of them are ready to pick up the microphone and take over. Don't be too quick to sign up someone simply because he or she has equipment and will work cheaply. If you are not able to actually hear and watch the person work, look for a recommendation from someone whose opinion you trust.

Between your collection of CDs, ones you can borrow from friends, and perhaps those that belong to the DJ, you will likely have a good music selection available to you. Don't hesitate to include any unique music you want. The thing is, don't simply rely on the DJ's choices. Listen to his recommendations to be sure they fit in with what you have in mind.

Taped music. Another possibility is to choose a selection of music that appeals to you, and to record it ahead of time on cassette tapes. Arrange the tapes in the order you want them played, and ask a friend to be in charge of seeing that they are played continually and in the proper order. (Be sure the person you ask is dependable. You will have enough to think about without worrying about why the music stopped.)

Double duty. If you hire a musician, ask what that person would charge to perform for both the ceremony and the reception. It costs less—often only about $100— to hire one person both for than to hire two separate musicians. Since many musicians play more than one instrument, you may even be able to treat your guests to more than one type of music.

Untapped local talent. The same types of local talent we discussed for your ceremony are possibilities for your reception. This could be an individual, an instrumentalist and a vocalist, a brass quartet, even a small band made up of local students.

With your wedding reception in mind, keep your eyes and ears open whenever you attend social functions. And be sure to let your friends know you are looking for talent. You will undoubtedly get a nice selection of leads.

Two last words. Next to the last word: When Sara Campbell married Colin McDougall, the featured musician was a bag-piper. Lois and Doug celebrated their Louisiana roots with a Cajun band. When Alicia married Gordon, who was from the beautiful Ozark mountains, their guests were entertained with a bluegrass band. A gospel pop vocalist sang at Sue and Patrick's reception. Your family traditions and background, and those of your fiancé, can be a wonderful part of your wedding celebration. The music you choose is a perfect way to personalize your reception.

And the last word: Many couples, especially those who have smaller or more casual receptions, have no music at all. In fact, there are some churches that don't even allow music. While music can add a lot, your reception, and even your ceremony, can be wonderfully successful without it.

The Reception Music Options chart (page 134) should help you determine which music option will work best for you. Then, when you have made a decision, use the next chart to lay out your reception music plan.

FLOWERS

The floral category is a large one that includes personal flowers, ceremony flowers, and flowers for the reception. Personal flowers are bouquets, boutonnieres, corsages, and perhaps hair pieces. Ceremony flowers include arrangements for the altar and possibly aisle decorations. At your reception, you may decide to use flowers as table and buffet centerpieces, and perhaps to decorate your wedding cake. On the average, brides spend around $500 for flowers, but the cost can soar to $2,000 or even more.

Is that you gasping? If the amount you have budgeted for flowers is far lower than that, don't worry. It is possible to cut your floral costs without scrimping noticeably. Here are some ways to do it:

Use free flowers. Depending on where you live and the time of year of your wedding, you may be able to get all your flowers and greenery donated or loaned. Susan, who lives in Washington state, decorated the reception hall for her fall

Reception Music Options ❧

OPTION 1 Music Plan: _____

__ Volunteer Musicians   __ Other Musicians   __ Pre-recorded Music

Contact Person: _____ Phone: _____

Equipment Needed: _____

Helpers Needed: _____

Notes: _____

_____

Cost: $ _____ Choice: __ Yes   __ No

OPTION 2 Music Plan: _____

__ Volunteer Musicians   __ Other Musicians   __ Pre-recorded Music

Contact Person: _____ Phone: _____

Equipment Needed: _____

Helpers Needed: _____

Notes: _____

_____

Cost: $ _____ Choice: __ Yes   __ No

OPTION 3 Music Plan: _____

__ Volunteer Musicians   __ Other Musicians   __ Pre-recorded Music

Contact Person: _____ Phone: _____

Equipment Needed: _____

Helpers Needed: _____

Notes: _____

_____

Cost: $ _____ Choice: __ Yes   __ No

Reception Music Plan ✤

	Phone	Cost
Musicians		
Contact Person		
	Total Cost	$
	Deposit Paid	$
	Balance Due	$

Description of Music Plan

_____

_____

_____

_____

_____

_____

_____

_____

_____

wedding in evergreen boughs, ferns, and flowering bushes loaned and arranged by friends of her family. For Julia's summer wedding, her aunt called upon friends and neighbors whose gardens were full of flowers, shrubs, and flowering bushes. How about your friends, relatives, and neighbors? Do they have gardens? How about the local garden club? Their members can be amazingly generous people, as Marcia found when she looked their number up in the telephone book and gave them a call.

Another possible source of free plants and shrubs is your local nursery. Many are willing to loan out a certain number of their plants at no charge. "I was able to borrow the most beautiful baskets of flowering azaleas," one young woman told us. "The church social hall looked like a spring garden. And all I did was ask at the nursery!"

Or you might want to call directly on Mother Nature herself. If you will be having a spring or summer wedding, keep your eyes open for fields of wildflowers. Annie, from Texas, added an interesting and delicate touch to her bouquets with sprigs of delicate blue lupine. Mary Jean used black-eyed Susans for the table centerpieces at her reception. Depending on where you live, you might want to watch for such lovely additions as Queen Anne's Lace, poppies, asters, or one of the several types of daisies. Ask a dependable friend to be in charge of gathering the flowers the day before your wedding, storing them in a cool place in lots of water (remind that person to rinse off any bugs or spiders that may be residing in the petals or leaves), and getting the bouquets to the church in plenty of time on the day of your wedding.

Wherever you get your flowers, choose those that are slightly closed so they won't be too full on your wedding day. Be especially careful to select tight rosebuds. If they are open, you can refrigerate them overnight with their stems in water. The cold will keep them from opening any further.

If your wedding is planned around a season such as Easter or Christmas, the church itself might be a source of free flowers. Joanna was married the Saturday before Palm Sunday, and the church was bedecked in palm branches and greenery. All she added was a bouquet of white gladiolus—which she bought by the stem at a grocery store—on either side of the altar.

So which flowers are acceptable for your wedding? You be the judge. Consider anything growing that strikes your fancy as fair game. You don't have to use traditional flowers. Janice allowed herself to be unique, and she ended up decorating with sunflowers from her father's Nebraska yard. The effect was stunningly beautiful.

Of course you will not be able to arrange a bunch of flowers at the last minute by yourself. Choose an artistic (and dependable!) friend to be in charge of the arranging, and others who can assist. Your volunteers will almost certainly have a great time putting it all together and setting up the arrangements on your wedding day.

Don't be afraid to let people know you are working on a budget and that you would welcome help. That's what Louetta did. Both she and her fiancé had children and full-time jobs which meant tight budgets and little spare time. "A close friend asked if, as a wedding gift, she could do our flowers," Louetta says. "She decorated my house—where the wedding was held—with pots of tulips and narcissus. And she made a bouquet of miniature white calla lilies and baby's breath for me, and a white rose boutonniere for my groom. What a wedding gift! I can't remember who gave me the glass platter or the wooden coasters, but I'll never forget who provided those beautiful flowers!"

Fine silks. What if you have no access to fresh flowers? Or if you just can't handle that "last minute" approach? Think silk! You will still need some filler foliage, but you can get that before the last minute, and it's available at a reasonable price almost anywhere at almost any time.

There are literally hundreds of silk flowers to choose from, and they are available in many places; craft shops and import outlet stores (such as Cost Plus or Pier 1 Imports) are good places to look. If you pick through the assortment of possibilities carefully, and if you're choosy, you will find beautiful flowers that look just like the real thing.

"But then I won't have real flowers at my wedding!" you might be saying.

Many brides consider that an advantage. If you are not one of them, you might want to supplement the silk flowers with a few real ones—the corsages for your mothers, for instance, or your bridal bouquet.

Sharing. Six weeks before her wedding, Lisa got a telephone call from a young woman by the name of Joanie. "I'm getting married in the gardens at five in the evening after your morning wedding," she said. "And I was wondering if you would like to do some sharing. If we shared the flowers, it would only cost each of us half as much."

Well, not really. They wouldn't be sharing the bridal bouquet, nor the attendants' bouquets. And Lisa certainly couldn't gather up the corsages and boutonnieres she had given out and pass them on to Joanie. The centerpiece on the reception table and a flower bedecked archway were all that really seemed sharable. Yet even that small amount helped.

Although it might be possible to transport the flowers to or from another site, it seems an awful lot of trouble for a small savings. The bride most likely to benefit from a sharing arrangement is one who is getting married in a church with a reception in the church social hall, and whose wedding follows or precedes another wedding on the same day, or at most the next day. But it is something to consider. Sharing just might work for you.

Do some yourself. One of the best ways to maximize your florist dollars is to order some of the flowers from a florist (your bouquet, the attendants' bouquets, the boutonnieres and corsages), then to put together the arrangements for the ceremony and reception. If you are able to get flowers for the arrangements donated, you will save approximately one third the usual cost. Not a bad savings. And it can spare you a lot of last minute work and worry.

Money-Saving Tips

- **Carry a Bible or prayer book in place of a bouquet.** That's what Kay did at her wedding. She used her sister's small white Bible and tied a white orchid and several sprigs of greenery on top with a satin ribbon and streamers. It was attractive, and particularly meaningful.

- **Stick with flowers that are in season.** If you buy out-of-season blooms, they are going to be expensive. (Red roses can more than quadruple in price in February!) If you depend on a volunteer to provide flowers out of season, the blossoms may not look as nice as you want—or worse, they may not even be open on your wedding day.

- **Recycle your ceremony flowers for your reception.** All you need to do is designate someone to unobtrusively transport them from the church to the reception site and place them in predetermined places.

- **Get double duty from the bridesmaids' bouquets.** Bridesmaids can place their bouquets in a designated flower holder on the bridal table at the reception. Besides making the table more attractive, this will relieve your bridesmaids of having to decide where to put their flowers during the reception.

- **Decorate the reception in unique ways.** Flowers are not your only option. Have you thought about balloons? "The balloon man virtually covered the place with red, white and blue balloons for our July wedding," Michelle recalls. "The only flowers we used were white mums on each serving table. We couldn't believe how far our decorating budget stretched."

Judy also used balloons—two hundred in assorted colors. ("The assorted were a lot cheaper than all one color," she says.) She rented a helium tank for $30, and her friends made a giant balloon arch over the auditorium entrance. There were enough balloons left to float around the large room, adding a festive touch and accenting the white carnations and purple irises on the tables.

Stephanie used pumpkins and oak branches for her October wedding in a park. Geneva used fruits and vegetables in straw cornucopias for her late November wedding. The possibilities are limited only by your imagination.

Getting some ideas of your own? Good for you! While they are still fresh in your mind, write them down. Do your planning on the Floral Needs chart, then use the Floral Plan Options chart to help you decide the plan that would work best for you.

PHOTOGRAPHY

Just about every couple wants pictures of their wedding. In fact, the average couple spends approximately $1,000 for professional wedding photography. And just what can you expect to get for that $1,000? Most photographers will shoot your wedding and take posed shots before or after the ceremony, then provide you with approximately 150 proofs

Floral Needs ❧

Qty		Ceremony Flowers	Cost
	Bride:	Bouquet	
	Bridal Attendants:	Honor Attendant's Bouquet	
		Bridesmaids' Bouquets	
		Flower Girls' Bouquets	
	Groom:	Groom's Boutonniere	
	Groomsmen:	Best Man's Boutonniere	
		Groomsmens' Boutonnieres	
		Ushers' Boutonnieres	
		Ring Bearer's Boutonniere	
	Family Members:	Mother of the Bride Corsage	
		Mother of the Groom Corsage	
		Grandmothers' Corsages	
		Boutonnieres for Men	
	Ceremony Site:	Candelabra	
		Candlelighters	
		Pew Decorations	
		Floral Spray	
		Potted Flowers	
		Potted Plants	
	Miscellaneous:	Soloists	
		Musicians	
		Guestbook Attendant	
		Wedding Coordinator	
		Servers	
	Reception Flowers:	Head Table Centerpiece	
		Serving Table Centerpiece	
		Table Centerpieces	
		Top of Cake	

Budgeted Amount: $_____

Total Cost: $_____

Floral Plan ❧

OPTION 1

Plan Description   __ Free/borrowed   Source: _____

                       __ Silks   Source: _____

                       __ Shared   Source: _____

                       __ Florist

Contact Person or Volunteer: _____

Phone: _____

Appointment Time: _____

Cost: $ _____

OPTION 2

Plan Description   __ Free/borrowed   Source: _____

                       __ Silks   Source: _____

                       __ Shared   Source: _____

                       __ Florist

Contact Person or Volunteer: _____

Phone: _____

Appointment Time: _____

Cost: $ _____

OPTION 3

Plan Description   __ Free/borrowed   Source: _____

                       __ Silks   Source: _____

                       __ Shared   Source: _____

                       __ Florist

Contact Person or Volunteer: _____

Phone: _____

Appointment Time: _____

Cost: $ _____

from which you can choose. You will receive your own album of pictures and possibly a bridal portrait.

"Hold it!" you may be saying. "Doesn't the cost of film and processing only come to about $.70 for each picture? That means the actual cost of that package should be about $100. So how come the photographer charges so much?"

Well, certainly there are other expenses, such as the photographic equipment and the photographer's overhead, but mostly what you are paying for is the photographer's labor. There is a lot to be said for having great pictures at your wedding, but there is also a lot to be said for staying within your budget. Can you do both? Absolutely! Read on.

Use an amateur photographer. If you have a friend or relative who takes great pictures, has a good camera, and is willing to photograph your wedding, you may want to go this route. With the cost of film, developing, and printing, you should be able to get approximately 100 pictures for around $70.

The brand of film you choose is not important, but the film speed is. ASA 200 is a good general purpose film. For a very bright day, 100 is better. If the pictures will be taken indoors, choose 400. You can have the photos printed in the 5x7, 4x6, or 3x5 inch size. Should people want extra copies, or a particular picture in a larger size, prints can be ordered later.

While drugstore processing is much less expensive than professional labs, the picture quality can be extremely disappointing, especially in the larger sizes. Even worse, the negatives may be damaged by less-than-careful handling. And if your film is not developed properly, you won't get another chance to try again. On a once-in-a-lifetime occasion such as your wedding, we strongly suggest you spring for the cost of a professional lab.

This is about the least expensive way of getting pictures of your wedding, but you must understand that it is also the most risky. If you are disappointed with the pictures, you can't go back and take them again. We have all seen those snapshots where everyone has their eyes closed, or the top of Aunt Mary's head is cut off, or the group is posed in front of a bush that makes it look as if limbs are growing out of everyone's head. Many brides have been disappointed with the photos shot by friends or family members who meant well but just weren't familiar with lighting considerations, perspectives, and angles, or who had no idea how to photograph people in a way that would accentuate their good traits and de-emphasize those they would like to forget.

If you're going to use an amateur photographer, we would suggest that you take two precautions: First, ask more than one person to take pictures, and provide each with film. With more photographers, you have greatly increased your chance of having a nice selection of good shots. **Second, provide your photographers with a list of shots that are really important to you.** One way to increase you chances of getting all those important shots is to arrange for an assistant who knows the names of family members. This person can get people together for the shots you want. The chart on page 146 will help you determine your "must shots."

Photography Tips

- **Pay attention to the background.** Try to snap your subject in uncluttered areas. Especially watch out for tree branches, flower arrangements, and other innocuous things that can end up looking like extra arms, or as if they are growing out of someone's head.

- **Be aware of the sun and shadows.** You don't want to have people facing into the sun where they will be squinting, but you don't want the sun behind them, either, or their faces will be in deep shade. The best thing to do is to use your flash to even out the lighting and get rid of the shadows. And do keep the light exposure uniform for the entire group of people being photographed—be careful not to have some in full sun while others are in shadow.

When photographing indoors, be careful that you don't underexpose. The bride's white dress can throw off your camera's light meter. When there is a broad expanse of white, turn off your camera's automatic feature and focus on the subject's face, then lock the setting. This way faces won't be underexposed.

- **Set your subjects up attractively.** Be creative in your posing. Your first inclination may be to stand everyone up in a straight line. Instead, group them in a more natural way. When they see the pictures they will appreciate your thoughtfulness in placing heavier and taller people in the back and smaller ones in front. Stairways are good settings for group shots. (There are examples of good and bad group placements on page 148.)

  You should always take two or three shots of important poses to be sure you get a good one. You are better off wasting a few shots than not getting the picture.

- **Look for special moments.** Two of the special shots caught by one amateur photographer were that of the mother of the bride and her sister holding hands, and of the groom's father giving last minute instructions to an intent flock of darling little flower girls. Keep an eye out for meaningful looks, telling touches, special hugs, and memorable moments. Don Æt be afraid to come in tight on a shot, framing only the faces.

- **During the ceremony, use the flash carefully.** Since some churches don't allow a flash in the sanctuary, it's a

Photographer's Checklist ✤

This list was compiled and given to us by a professional wedding photographer. Listed are some of his favorite and most popular poses. Look at this list as a starting point for your own creativity.

✓	**Before the Ceremony**
	Bride getting ready
	Bride alone
	Bride with bridesmaids
	Groom alone
	Groom with parents
	Guests arriving
	Ushers seating special guests
	Guests signing guestbook

✓	**During the Ceremony**
	Seating of bride's parents
	Seating of groom's parents
	Entrance of minister
	Entrance of groom
	Entrance of groomsmen
	Entrance of flower girl/ringbearer
	Entrance of bridesmaids
	Entrance of bride
	Father giving bride away
	Special musicians
	Soloists
	Lighting of unity candle
	Wedding party during ceremony
	Bride and groom saying vows
	Bride and groom's kiss
	Recessional

✓	**After the Ceremony**
	Bride alone
	Groom alone
	Bride with honor attendant
	Groom with best man
	Bride with bridesmaids
	Groom with groomsmen
	Bride with groomsmen
	Groom with bridesmaids
	Bridesmaids only
	Groomsmen only
	Flower girl
	Ring bearer
	Entire wedding party
	Bride with her parents
	Groom with his parents
	Bride and groom with all parents
	Immediate families
	Extended families
	Special friends

✓	**Special Events**
	Cutting the cake
	Toasts
	Throwing the bouquet/garter
	Bride and groom leaving

good idea to check ahead of time. Even if you can use the flash, do so only during the processional and the recessional. During the service use natural light with timed exposures.

- **Take as many pictures as possible before the ceremony begins.** The more shots on the couple's "must" list you can do beforehand, the less pressure you'll have between the ceremony and the reception.

Posing Suggestions

Whether your wedding photographer is a seasoned professional or an amateur hobbyist, you want your pictures to look perfect. Ask your photographer to do some creative posing, especially with those big group shots.

The temptation when photographing large families or the entire wedding party is to make them stand in a long, single file line. Boring!

Why not try something more interesting and creative like using stairs or steps to break up that monotonous line? It's okay to place some people sitting or kneeling in front.

Amateur photographer plus studio portraits. If it is important to you to have professional portraits, you can supplement your amateur photographers' work by going to a studio either before or after your wedding and having a professional portrait made. While this option will cost you more money (approximately $125 for an eight-by-ten portrait), you'll have the advantage of professional quality.

Combo approach. A good compromise that can save you quite a bit of money is to have a professional photographer shoot just the ceremony and portraits, then have an amateur shoot the reception. You can then buy prints from the photographer and put your album together yourself. (Many photographers charge by the hour with a two-hour minimum. One photographer quoted a charge of $650 for this plan as opposed to an estimated $1,125 for her full service with a completed leather album.)

A pro shoots, you develop. Sometimes a professional photographer will agree to a plan where he or she brings the equipment and film to shoot the wedding, then leaves the film with someone designated by the bride, who in turn has it processed at a professional lab. You get the advantage of having a professional wedding photographer who is using his or her own camera and film. While this will cost you quite a bit more than if you go the amateur route, it is less expensive than hiring a full-service professional to do it all. (The average quote we got for this service was $500 for two hours of shooting on 35-millimeter film.)

Since not all photographers are willing to work this way, you will have to ask around to find those who are. Then check their work to be sure you are happy with the finished product.

Shop around. If you decide to use a professional photographer, be sure to take the time and trouble to shop around—early! Photographers' prices vary considerably, as do their experience and expertise. **Ask each prospective photographer**:

- How many hours will you spend photographing the wedding for the price you are quoting?

- When will the preview pictures be ready for us to see?

- Does the price include an album?

- If so, which album?

- Exactly how many photos will be included and what size will they be?

- When will the photographs arrive?

- May I see samples of your work?

- May I have the names and telephone numbers of references?

Always get everything in writing. Many photographers will have preprinted price and information sheets. If the photographer is offering you something other than what is printed up, have him or her write out the plan, and date and sign it. This will not only help keep the photographer honest, but it will protect you from misunderstandings.

Be prepared for heavy pressure from photographers.

For instance, many professionals will push their own packages, which usually include an album that they assemble for you. This is the most profitable option for them, and, as you might imagine, the most expensive for you. Don't be afraid to suggest other options ("We will be getting and arranging our own album. All we need are the pictures. How much will you charge for that?") Refuse to be pressured into making quick decisions. If one photographer won't be flexible and accommodating to your needs, keep looking until you find someone who is.

A few final words of advice. To get the names of possible photographers, ask recently married couples and wedding coordinators for recommendations. You can also inquire at bridal shows sponsored by bridal shops or department stores. The *worst* way to find a photographer is to look in the phone book. Anyone who has a telephone can be listed there, and anyone can buy an advertisement.

Don't be shy about discussing fees with a photographer. Ask if there are packages with different prices. And be on the alert for hidden costs. If your package comes with an album, for instance, be sure you see the *actual album* you are to receive. Some photographers show sample photos in beautiful leather albums. When you get yours in a cheap vinyl album, the photographer quickly announces, "Of course, the leather would be much nicer. For an extra charge I can...."

If you choose your own album, watch out for plastic pages that are not PVC-free plastic. Over time, the chemicals in them can damage your prints. Albums with pockets for pictures are better for your photos than those with sticky pages, but they are also much more expensive. A nice alternative is an album with pages on which you can attach tab corners into which you can slip the corners of your prints.

Budget Tips

- The trend is toward more candid shots and fewer posed photographs. This is good news for brides who choose to use amateur photographers.

- Don't be prejudiced against a photographer who doesn't work out of a studio. If you hire one who works from home, you will likely save between 20 and 40 percent.

- Skip the extra frills. Those gift folios touted as "the perfect gift for the members of your wedding party" can add an enormous expense to your budget. And instead of the formal portraits the photographer will insist no bride can do without, consider blowing up a good candid shot. Don't order frames or albums from the photographer, either. The markup is staggering.

- If you can possibly get all the photo copies you want at one time, you may be able to get a quantity discount.

VIDEOTAPING

Although videography is relatively new—it has only been around since the 1980s—it has become very popular with brides and grooms. No wonder. Just pop the videotape into your videocassette player and you can relive the wonder of your wedding day any time you want! But, yes, it is another expense to add to your budget.

Although the cost of a professional videotape can be as low as $250 or as high as $2,500, the average is between $500 and $800.

All kinds of things can be incorporated into a videotape: a photo montage of baby pictures of the two of you, interviews with members of the wedding party and guests at the reception, a visit to your home on the day of the wedding, special editing, graphics, commentary—the possibilities are endless. Of course, the more frills added and the more editing involved, the more expensive the video. You can figure that each special touch will add an extra $100 to $500 to the overall cost.

As with a photographer, the best way to locate a good videographer is to ask for references from recently married couples, wedding photographers, and ceremony site coordinators, and to inquire at bridal shows.

Photographer Estimates ❧

OPTION 1:

Photographer: _____

Address: _____

Phone: _____

Plan Description:

__ Amateur __ Amateur plus studio portraits

__ Professional shots, self-developed __ Professional

__ Professional at wedding, amateur at reception

Total Cost: $ _____ Deposit Required: _____

Price Includes: _____

_____

OPTION 2:

Photographer: _____

Address: _____

Phone: _____

Plan Description:

__ Amateur __ Amateur plus studio portraits

__ Professional shots, self-developed __ Professional

__ Professional at wedding, amateur at reception

Total Cost: $ _____ Deposit Required: _____

Price Includes: _____

_____

Photographer Estimates, continued

OPTION 3:

Photographer: _____

Address: _____

Phone: _____

Plan Description:

    __ Amateur   __ Amateur plus studio portraits

    __ Professional shots, self-developed __ Professional

    __ Professional at wedding, amateur at reception

Total Cost: $ _____   Deposit Required: _____

Price Includes: _____

"But my Uncle Bob has a video camera," you may be saying. "He said he would record the wedding for me for nothing!"

Good point. And that brings us to the first of our options to the high cost of professional videotaping.

Use an amateur. If you have a friend or relative with a quality video camera who is willing to tape your wedding, you can get a video for just the price of the blank videotape (which should be the finest quality available, by the way). Before you settle on a particular amateur videographer, try to watch some videotapes he or she has made.

Should two or three people offer to record your wedding day, take them all up on it. If you have more than one camera taping the ceremony, each could tape from a different perspective, perhaps one from the front corner and another from the rear. Your only additional cost would be the price of the extra tapes.

Understand that, unlike a professional videographer, your amateur won't give you an edited tape. Nor will you get any of the extra touches and frills. But then, you won't get the huge bill, either. And because it is relatively easy to videotape, there is a good chance that you will end up with an acceptable record of your special day. With videotaping, there is no arranging or posing or positioning needed. All the videographer has to do is tape the wedding and reception as they happen.

Volunteer Videographer, Rented Camera. What if you have a volunteer you feel would do a good job but who has no camera? Simple—rent one! You can rent a quality camera for less than $50. Be sure you also get a tripod to keep the camera steady. And you will want to rent two fully-charged battery packs.

If you do have an amateur videographer record your wedding, help ensure that the end results will be satisfying by giving the following list of tips to that person.

Videotaping Tips

- **Move the camera smoothly.** Do your best to keep all the camera movements as slow and smooth as possible. If it seems to you that you are panning at a reasonable speed, you are almost certainly moving too quickly. To avoid jerks and bounces, use the tripod as often as you can. Be especially careful when you zoom in and out. Exaggerate your efforts to do it slowly and smoothly.

- **Get closeups.** Some wide-angle shots are fine, but it's the close-ups that really make the video personal. A good rule of thumb is to hold the camera on each shot to at least a count of five. At the time it will seem too long, but on tape it will be perfect.

- **Plan out interviews.** That word of advice from Grandma, the recollection of a grade school teacher, best wishes from the minister, messages from friends, your boss, the best man, the maid of honor. Spontaneous comments from the bride and groom. In the years to come, it is these interviews the bride and groom will enjoy again and again. But good interviews don't just happen. Think ahead of time about what you will ask. Instead of ambiguous questions ("Do you have anything to say to the new couple?") ask questions that invite sharing ("How did you first meet Michael?" "Do you have a special memory about Tanya?" "What words of advice do you have for the bride and groom?" "What will you especially remember about this wedding?") You may even want to write out your questions ahead of time so that you won't suddenly go blank at the reception. Ask the bride and groom if they have people they would especially like you to talk to, or questions they would like to have asked.

- **Have a dry run.** Not only do you want to be sure the camera is working properly, but it will help if you get in some practice recording. If you get a feel ahead of time for the speed at which you should move the camera, you won't have to worry about how you are doing on the real day.

- **Tape on the "sp" mode.** The two-hour speed will give you a much better picture than the longer play speed. But since you won't get as much on the film at this faster speed, be sure to have an extra videotape with you.

- **Be "invisible".** Don't allow yourself to become one of those overbearing videographers who feels he or she has to be the attention-getting life-of-the-party, always poking the camera in everyone's faces. Stay in the background.

- **Be an equal opportunity videographer.** It's easy to keep coming back to the person or people who interest you most (the beautiful bridesmaid, for instance, or your darling little granddaughter). But remember that the bride and groom will want to see and hear from a wide variety of their guests. Resist the temptation to zero in on your personal favorite.

Avoiding pitfalls.

Before you engage the services of a professional videographer, ask to see a demo tape. Not just highlights, but the *whole tape.* Watch for harsh lighting, listen for the quality of the sound, be aware of interviews where the guests look uncomfortable. How about the editing? Is it smooth and professional, or does it feel an awful lot like a home movie? And, once again, be sure to ask for references.

If you are using an amateur videographer, it is better to have one who will tape the wedding for you. Some people may tape the wedding for themselves and agree to give you a copy, but they will be following their own agenda rather than yours.

Whoever the videographer, be sure he or she knows the key elements you want recorded. Here are some video highlight suggestions:

- Interviews with friends, family members, the wedding party, and the bride and groom.

- Close-ups of any especially important guests, family members, and participants.

- Special events such as the bouquet toss, garter toss, cutting the cake, the reception line, special music, toasts and speeches, and the bride and groom leaving for their honeymoon.

Music, flowers, photographs, videotape. We have taken care of some important things in this chapter. Now get ready to plan the ceremony.

CHAPTER SEVEN

The Wedding Ceremony

All the planning, all the lists, all the organization—here is where they pay off. Your wedding ceremony, the pledging of your vows, is what it's all about. Everything that comes before is mere preparation. The rest of the day is just celebration. It's the ceremony that is the real thing.

Are you ready for some good budget news? Here it is: While the considerations in this chapter are very important, unlike just about every other area of your wedding, they are going to put little pressure on your budget.

Whether you will be acting as your own wedding coordinator or not, it is most important that you carefully think through the ceremony you want. Do you want traditional? Liturgical? Casual? Short and sweet? Long and formal? It's up to you and your fiancé.

The person officiating at your wedding will undoubtedly have model ceremonies for you to consider. Look at the suggestions, but see them for what they are—possibilities for you to think about. There are many different ways for you to personalize your ceremony. Here are some areas you might want to consider:

THE PROCESSIONAL

Who will walk you down the aisle? While the father of the bride is the traditional choice, you may prefer someone else—your brother, perhaps, or your step-father, your son, or an uncle. Or it may be that you prefer to walk along unaccompanied.

Will you be "given away"? Many older brides, or women who have been married before, feel foolish being given away by their fathers. As a matter of fact, more and more brides are choosing to rework this ancient tradition that they feel has lost its relevance in today's world. Some brides have their fathers walk them down the aisle, then their fathers sit down. Others choose to be given away by their mothers and fathers together. Some skip the whole thing. You decide what is appropriate for you.

THE CEREMONY

How about your vows? You can write your own vows, but you certainly don't have to. If you decide to go with the vows your minister has for you, be sure to read them over. Should you want some changes, don't hesitate to ask. Most ministers will be flexible to a certain extent.

Your other decision will be whether to recite your vows or to repeat them after the minister. The spontaneous feel of reciting them is certainly nice, but having to memorize your vows on top of all the other pressures of your wedding day may not be worth it. Also, you will run the risk of your mind suddenly going blank at the crucial moment. If you do decide to memorize the vows and recite them, be sure the minister has a copy of exactly what you intend to say so that he or she can help you along if you or your groom should need it.

Special features? Just about anything that helps make your wedding day special, personal, and meaningful is acceptable, so long as it is in keeping with the mood of the day. (We have to admit we would suggest you think long and hard before choosing your dog as the ring bearer, although it has been done!) Readings can be a nice touch—a favorite passage from the Bible, perhaps, or a special poem. You might even choose to have a touching or meaningful statement read at the ceremony from someone dear to you.

A popular wedding ceremony feature is the lighting of a unity candle, signifying the joining of two lives into one. At the beginning of the ceremony, two candles burn while a taller unlit candle stands between them. At the end of the ceremony, after the couple has been pronounced husband and wife, the bride and groom pick up their individual candles and together light the middle unity candle.

Special solos or musical numbers can be ceremony features. So can ethnic or religious traditions. (One bride and groom celebrated their African heritage in a moving traditional recitation; another couple incorporated an early Orthodox Christian wreath headpiece and incense ceremony into their wedding.)

Many couples find it especially meaningful to have a portion of Scripture read. One favorite is the passage from Ruth 1:16-17: "Where you go I will go, and where you stay I will stay. Your people will be my people and your God my God. Where you die I will die, and there I will be buried. May the Lord deal with me, be it ever so severely, if anything but death separates you and me." Another is the passage in 1 Corinthians 13 that ends with, "Now these three remain: faith, hope, and love. But the greatest of these is love."

Ways to include family and friends. Besides participating in the wedding party, special people can serve as candlelighters, one might offer a prayer, one might be in charge of the guest book, another might take charge of gifts that are brought to the ceremony and be sure the cards are taped on. These services will add a lot to your day, and it will mean a lot to you to have these special people as participants.

Your ceremony can be anything from an informal affair with a short meditation all the way to a formal service with a full-length sermon. Certainly you should ask the minister what he or she is planning to say to see if it agrees with what you have in mind.

Your ceremony is the perfect place for you to acknowledge your faith, and to express your spiritual convictions and your relationship with God. It is an opportunity for you to publicly reflect upon your faith and its place in your union, and to ask your guests to join you in asking God's blessing on your new life together.

To help you design just the right ceremony for you, we have included a ceremony worksheet. This is followed by a ceremony information sheet for your wedding coordinator.

The Ceremony ✣

Activity	Participant	Description
Prelude		
Processional *(Order of participants)*		
Welcome		
Reading or Prayer		
Music		
Wedding Meditation		
Giving of Bride *(Declaration of Consent)*		
Reading or Prayer		
Introduction to the Vows		
Bride's Vows		
Groom's Vows		

The Ceremony, continued

Activity	Participant	Description
Exchange of Rings		
Blessing of Rings		
Pronouncement of Union		
Music		
Prayer		
Special Acts of Celebration (Unity Candle, Communion)		
Benediction and Blessing		
Presentation of Couple		
Recessional		

Notes:

Wedding Coordinator's Ceremony Information ❧

	Arrival Time	Home Phone	Work Phone
Wedding Date and Time			
Rehearsal Date and Time			
Bride			
Groom			
Minister			
Ceremony Site Contact Person			
Honor Attendant			
Best Man			
Musicians			
Florist			
Rental Suppliers			
Photographer			
Videographer			
Guest Book Attendant			
Wedding Day Transportation			

SPECIAL PROPS

Props can do a lot to establish and enhance the mood of your wedding ceremony. And they are not expensive! (Although they can be difficult to assemble at the last minute.) We have listed some of the props you might want to consider:

Ceremony programs. Many couples like to have programs that give the order of the ceremony and identify the participants. Some also include information about the bride and groom and their families; words to songs, readings, or special poems; or an explanation or history of special ethnic or religious traditions. The program is a perfect place to record a favorite or especially appropriate passage of scripture, such as Psalm 23 or the great love chapter, 1 Corinthians 13.

You can design your program on a computer, then print copies and fold them yourself. Depending on how many you need, this sould not add more than$20 or so to your budget. But programs are by no means necessary. It probably isn't worth the cost of ordering them through a printer.

Candles. Candles at the altar add a lovely touch. Although candelabras can be rented through florists and other wedding supply establishments, many churches have sets that can be used at weddings. Be sure to ask what is available.

Some brides choose candles for pew decorations, but that can be a fire hazard. (We know of one bride whose veil caught fire as she walked up the aisle!) Candles can also be carried by the bridesmaids instead of—or as part of—their bouquets, although lighted candles can be difficult to handle.

If you decide to use a unity candle, you need not buy a special candle holder. Lisa used three brass candleholders she had received as wedding gifts. Other brides simply borrow crystal, silver, brass, or glass holders.

Although there are lovely hand-dipped candles in all colors

and textures and styles available at gift shops, drug and discount stores offer perfectly fine candles in just about every color imaginable for a much lower price.

Pillow for the ring bearer. If you plan to have a ring bearer, you can borrow a pillow from a former bride, or you can rent one. Or you can make the pillow yourself. It isn't hard to do, nor is it expensive. If you decide to make your own pillow, the following instructions will show you how to do it.

Make Your Own Ring Bearer's Pillow
A ring bearer's pillow is another surprisingly easy and inexpensive prop to make.

1. Start with a pillow form, available at any fabric store. Choose a size that you like; six to ten inches square is standard.
2. Cut out two fabric squares, two inches larger than the size of the pillow form. If you've chosen a six-by-six-inch pillow, cut eight-by-eight-inch squares.
3. On a sewing machine or by hand, stitch the two squares of fabric to each other. The side of the fabric that you want to show should be facing in when you do this. Leave an unstitched portion that is big enough to squeeze the pillow form through.
4. Turn the fabric so that the right side is facing out. Iron it so that the side seams are smooth. Put the pillow form inside and carefully sew the unstitched portion closed.
5. Decorate the pillow with lace, ribbons, bows, pearls, or any other pretty things you may find.
6. On the front of the pillow sew a piece of ribbon that is long enough to tie into a bow. This bow is to hold your rings. If your ring bearer is very young, you may opt to tie on false rings instead of the real ones.

Whatever pillow you use, if the ring bearer is very young it's a good idea to stitch two ribbon loops onto the underside for him to slide his hands into. That way you won't have to worry about him dropping the pillow on his way up the aisle.

Basket for the flower girl. This is a fairly easy one. If you order it through a florist, you will pay a lot more than if you get it yourself. Around Easter, you will find a wide assortment of white, straw, or pastel Easter baskets available. Or you can find baskets in the floral sections of many discount stores and at craft shops. You can fill the basket with petals for the flower girl to strew in your path, or she can simply carry a basket of flowers. One little girl's mother filled her basket with wild alyssum that she gathered the morning of the wedding. It was lovely, and so fragrant.

You can record the props you are considering on the Special Ceremony Props worksheet. Don't limit your ideas to the things we have suggested here. And don't hesitate to use things you have seen and liked in other weddings.

THE COMFORT OF YOUR GUESTS

If you are married in a church, you probably won't have to worry about this. (As long as you don't invite too many more guests than the church can comfortably seat, that is. One bride who was married in the chapel at her college ended up with guests standing outside trying to look in the windows!) But if you are married at home, or outside, you will need to give special thought to the comfort of your guests.

Seating. For a short ceremony inside a home, you can get by with limited seating as long as there is somewhere for guests who are elderly or who have disabilities to sit down. For a

Special Ceremony Props ✤

Programs

Printed by: _____

Address: _____ Phone: _____

Quantity: _____ Cost: $ _____

Deposit: $ _____

Balance Due: $ _____

Elements that require props	Props needed
Processional	
Candlelighting	
Music	
Exchange of vows	
Exchange of rings	
Recessional	

Props needed	Quantity	Cost	Color	Borrowed	Rented	Own
Candles						
Candleholders						
Ring Bearer's Pillow						
Flower Girl's Basket						

longer ceremony, or for a ceremony held outdoors, you will need to supply seating for all your guests. (The exception is when the ceremony is very short or casual enough for the guests to sit on the ground.)

You may be able to borrow chairs from your church or club, in which case you will need to arrange to have them moved to the wedding site, set up, and taken down after the ceremony. If this isn't possible, you can rent chairs. If you do rent, be sure you understand whether or not the cost includes setting them up and taking them down again. If it doesn't, you will need to round up helpers. (This is a good job for preteen or teenage relatives, but you should get an adult to oversee and guide their work.)

The sound system. Again, if you are married in a church, this will most likely be supplied. If the ceremony is held in a private home, you probably won't need it. But for an outside wedding, a sound system is important. It's frustrating to guests when they can't hear what is going on. And, yes, unless you can borrow a system it is going to cost you. The cost will depend on what you need: amplifiers, speakers, microphones, and so forth. To find an adequate sound system at the best price, look in the Yellow Pages under "Sound Systems" and "Music Stores," then start doing some comparative shopping.

Parking. Does the ceremony site you have selected have sufficient parking for your guests? Check it out. If the parking area isn't located in an obvious place (as is the case with some parks), let your guests know where to find it. (You can post a sign or include a map with your invitation.) If the parking is limited, you may want to suggest that your guests share rides. It may even be necessary to arrange a "shuttle" service or to provide volunteer "valets."

Facilities for those with disabilities. It's easy to overlook people with special needs. If you are inviting guests with disabilities, be sure that there are proper facilities for them—parking, seating, restrooms, and wheelchair access.

Your beautiful and meaningful ceremony will make the wedding of your dreams a reality. Now you are ready to make the reception plans that will polish off your perfect day.

CHAPTER EIGHT

The Reception

Friends and food and music and fun and toasts and a beautiful cake! Sound like the reception you have in mind? "It's what I want," you may be saying, "but my budget says 'no way!'"

Well, we say, "Don't take no for an answer!" You *can* have it all—more or less.

You might want to check how you are doing on your budget, and, if you are considering a high-priced place such as a restaurant or club house, to perhaps rethink your choice. It may indeed be the right place for you, or it could be that you will be just as happy in a less costly location. For instance, there are affordable sites available to you simply because you are a citizen of your community—parks, public gardens, museum grounds, local recreation centers, and local college and public school campuses. Or you may want to reconsider a home reception. Statistics show that fully 10 to 20 percent of all wedding receptions are now being held at home.

Where you decide to hold your reception is just the first of many decisions you will be making for this celebration. The Reception Worksheet will help you make specific plans.

The Reception ❦

RECEPTION SITE:

Contact Person: _____ Phone: _____

Coordinator: _____ Phone: _____

Planned Time: from: _____ to: _____

SITE AVAILABLE FOR DECORATING:

Coordinator: _____ Phone: _____

from: _____ to: _____

RENTAL EQUIPMENT:

Contact Person: _____ Phone: _____

Pick-Up ____   Delivery ____

when: _____ by whom: _____

TABLE/CHAIR SETUP:

when: _____ by whom: _____

CAKE PICK-UP/DELIVERY:

Contact Person: _____ Phone: _____

when: _____ by whom: _____

FLOWERS:

Contact Person: _____ Phone: _____

Pick-Up _____ Delivery _____

when: _____ by whom: _____

MUSICIANS:

Contact Person: _____ Phone: _____

Arrival: _____

CATERER:

Contact Person: _____ Phone: _____

Arrival: _____

HELPERS:

_____ Phone: _____

_____ Phone: _____

_____ Phone: _____

_____ Phone: _____

CLEANUP CREW:

_____ Phone: _____

_____ Phone: _____

_____ Phone: _____

_____ Phone: _____

Reception Checklist ❧

This list should start you thinking about all the factors to consider as you plan your reception.

✓	The Site	✓	Necessary Equipment
	Cost		Tent
	Distance from ceremony site		Chairs
	Easy for guests to find		Tables
	Decorating freedom and flexibility		Place settings
	Other receptions the same day?		Utensils
	Guest capacity		Glasses
	Insurance needed		Punch bowl
	Sufficiently staffed		Table coverings
	Good refund policy		Dance floor
	No hidden costs		Sound system
	Parking availability		DJ equipment
	Clean restrooms		Serving trays
	Changing rooms		Platters
	Handicapped access		Lighting

✓	Food and Drink	✓	Miscellaneous
	Food is allowed		Musicians
	Food is available		Florist
	Flexibility in food preparation		Photographer
	Price per guest		Videographer
	Total cost		Cake server and knife
	Wedding cake served as dessert		Toasting glasses for couple
	Alcoholic beverages allowed		Guest book
	Cost to provide alcohol		Gift table
	Cost of non-alcoholic drinks		Seating arrangements
	Cost for bartender service		Place cards
	Cost for servers		Favors
	Food available for service people		

Notes:

A very important decision—and one that has the potential of breaking your budget, by the way—is the selection of food and drink you will serve to your guests.

ABOUT THE MENU

Many brides insist, "Whether I can afford it or not, I have to serve some sort of meal. I mean, our guests will expect it, won't they?" That's a good question. Just what *will* your guests be expecting in the way of food? To a degree, it depends on the time of day your wedding is held. Here is a general guideline of what is appropriate:

Morning Reception (Before 11 A.M.):
- Continental Breakfast
- Breakfast Buffet
- Snacks

Midday Reception (11 A.M. to 1 P.M.)
- Luncheon Buffet

Afternoon Reception (1 P.M. to 4 P.M.)
- Hors d'oeuvres
- Cake and Punch

Early Evening Reception (4 P.M. to 7 P.M.)
- Dinner Buffet

Evening Reception (After 7 P.M.)
- Hor d'oeuvres
- Cake and Punch

Since an afternoon or evening reception will require the least amount of food, it will be the least expensive to host. Yet within every time frame, there are ways to maximize your reception budget.

If you hire a caterer, he or she will handle everything for you—food, drinks, rentals, cleanup, perhaps even the flowers. It's convenient to be sure, but it can also be expensive. To determine whether or not a caterer will fit into your reception budget, call several and tell them, "I would like to have a reception for (give the number of guests), and I plan to spend (give a specific amount of money). What can you do for that price?" If the caterer can offer you a plan you like, great. If not, keep reading. You have a lot of options.

All in the family. Whatever your wedding plans, from buffet dinner to cake and punch only, relying on your family will be your least expensive option. Here is how it works: Family and friends prepare the foor for your reception, and donate the ingredients in the dishes. It used to be that this was the way most wedding receptions were put together.

You and a relative or friend should decide on a menu and determine who should bring what. The people who prepare the food can also store it until the day of the wedding. Besides providing the prepared food, your volunteers may be willing to help serve, and perhaps to even help clean up afterward. (Or you may decide to arrange for another clean-up crew.)

To make it easier on your volunteers, and to ensure that your buffet table has an attractive, uniform look rather than the thrown-together look of a potluck supper, it's a good idea to plan out and organize the serving table. Start by making a diagram of the buffet table as you would like it to look at reception time. If you are providing the serving bowls and platters, tape a small pice of paper to each indicating what is to be served in it: fruit salad, cheese platter, sandwiches, and so forth. You can even place an appropriate serving utensil with each platter and bowl.

Even though you will have lots of willing hands to help you, designate someone reliable to be in charge of the kitchen. Ask another person to oversee the refreshment table to make sure that the platters and bowls are kept filled and that the table doesn't begin to look picked over. Ask a third person to be in charge of pouring and serving the drinks.

The cake and beverage reception. This is an easy and inexpensive type of reception. Besides the wedding cake, which is the center of attention on the reception table, all you need to provide is paper products, drinks (coffee, tea, and punch), and mints and nuts.

The best of two worlds. If you can afford to spend more, and you have willing volunteers to help, you can have the test of two worlds. You can purchase the main dishes while all the side dishes are provided by family and friends.

When family and friends ask you if they can do anything to help, answer, "As a matter of fact, there is." Then pull out your list of side dishes and ask what they would like to contribute. You will be surprised at how many people are ready and willing to be a part of your reception preparations.

Willing hands buffet. A hot buffet is the perfect answer to the budget-conscious bride whose wedding time calls for a full meal. Whether it's breakfast, lunch, or dinner, willing hands can turn out a wonderful spread at an affordable price.

When you are planning your menu, keep in mind that the less that has to be done at the last minute, the better. Also, the less meat your menu calls for, the less expensive your meal will likely be.

If you purchase the majority of your food ahead at whole-sale food service suppliers (warehouses that sell to the public as well as to restaurants and catering services) you will be surprised at how much farther your food dollars will stretch. Warehouse clubs such as Sam's Club or Price Club also have excellent prices. You can also check for good prices on fresh platters at local supermarkets.

For Lisa's reception after her 10 A.M. wedding, we purchased four packages of frozen mini quiches that only needed to be popped into the microwave (forty-eight quiches for $7.99 at a warehouse club). At the supermarket we bought two large platters of beautiful fresh vegetables attractively arranged around a hollowed-out purple cabbage filled with dip ($32 for platters serving up to thirty-six people), and one large platter piled high with an assortment of luscious fruit ($42 for approximately forty servings). The table was rounded out with dishes of mixed nuts, mints, and Hershey's Kisses, all of which we bought in bulk at the wholesale grocery warehouse. Of course we served cake, punch, and coffee and tea as well. Even with two hundred guests in attendance, there was food left over.

Our local wholesale grocery offers such buys as ten-pound packages of turkey breast for $17.95, five-pound containers of fruit ambrosia for $4.50, four-pound bags of frozen meatballs for $6.49, and six-pound frozen lasagnas for $9.50. There are excellent bulk buys on coffee, tea, punch concentrate, and wine as well.

With planning, searching out good buys, and the willing hands of your friends, your buffet reception can be a great success.

Use the church's food service. Churches often have social halls for wedding receptions held after church ceremonies, usually for a small fee. Some provide all the accessories you will need: table cloths, silverware, china, candle holders, coffee urns, punch bowls, even platters and serving items. If you need anything that isn't provided, you may be able to borrow it from someone. Or you can look for serving pieces at wholesale food suppliers. (We found nice looking crystal-cut pattern plastic trays priced as low as $2.99, bowls as low as $1.99, and 12-quart punch bowls for $7.99.)

Some churches have a food service staff that will prepare food and serve it at the reception. There is a wide variety in the menus they offer—everything from cold cuts and cheese platters, to fruit and salad buffets, to sit-down dinners. Some groups even offer certain ethnic dishes! If such a service is available at the church where you will be married, ask about it, the menus, and what the cost will be.

Have an informal reception. This type of reception is perfect for an early afternoon wedding. Only a few chairs and tables are necessary as most people want to walk around and mingle anyway. Although there needn't be a buffet table, some light refreshments should be available. The wedding cake is the highlight of the occasion.

Or perhaps a really casual reception. A reception doesn't have to be a formal affair.

Maggie, a young Texas bride, wanted her large family of brothers, sisters, nieces, nephews, cousins, aunts, and uncles—as well as their friends of all ages—all to enjoy her reception in the meadow of the lovely wooded park where she was married. So they had a Texas-style barbecue that culminated in a soccer game for the kids (which ended up including just about everyone under forty!).

"We had 150 people," Maggie said, "and the bill was only $300. Everyone wanted to help, everyone wanted to celebrate, everyone wanted to play soccer, and everyone had fun!"

Casual receptions are becoming more and more popular, and it's no wonder. They can be done reasonably, and they can be great fun for everyone.

Perhaps more than in any other part of your wedding, your reception can reflect you and your new husband, and the things that make you unique and special. Formal or casual, large or small, make your wedding reception what you want it to be.

Even though Marilyn and Brad knew that the majority of their budget would be going toward their honeymoon trip, they wanted their reception to be a wonderful time of celebration, too. Their planning and careful preparations may help you as you plan your own reception.

Marilyn and Brad began by sitting down with a legal pad and a pencil and making notes. How many people would they invite? (About one hundred, they decided.) What time of day would it be? (2 P.M. to 5 P.M.) What utensils and appliances would they need to prepare the food? "We listed everything we could think of," Marilyn says, "from food to serving table to trash bags." Then they divided their list into four sections: what they could borrow, what they would rent or buy, who they could count on as volunteers, and who they would have to hire.

"We decided to have the wedding cake professionally made," Marilyn says. "For the rest of the food, we called on a dozen friends who had asked if there was anything they could do to help." Marilyn noted that several friends had complained that they didn't know what to give as wedding gifts since both she and Brad had been living independently for a number of years. "I told them that what we really needed was their time and their best recipes."

Once the helpers were chosen, Marilyn invited them all over for lunch and a marathon planning session. The menu was what Marilyn terms "filling hors d'oeuvres." One of Marilyn's volunteers offered to prepare her specialty—stuffed mushrooms. Another committed herself to bowls of crab dip. Another volunteered her mother's recipe for homemade salsa and chips. Yet another said she would be in charge of fruit kabobs. "We looked for special dishes that could be made in advance, ones that complemented each other yet featured a variety of flavors and colors," Marilyn said.

They estimated that each guest would eat eight hors d'oeuvres, so they would need eight hundred hors d'oeuvres.

Then they divided that eight hundred by the twelve volunteers, which meant each volunteer was responsible for preparing sixty-seven servings.

On the day of the wedding, each volunteer delivered her dish in a disposable container between the hours of 11 A.M. and noon to the park site where the reception would be held. Marilyn's sister-in-law, who was chosen to act as coordinator, waited there and checked each dish off on her master checklist.

Brad volunteered his friends to take charge of the soft drinks and to make coffee.

Everyone who attended Marilyn's and Brad's reception agreed that it was one of the best they had ever attended. "We think our close friends especially enjoyed it, because they did so much to help make it a success."

A FEW MORE WORDS OF RECEPTION ADVICE

It is vitally important that you have someone in charge of your reception—*not* you, your mother, or any other member of your wedding party. (This is a lesson we learned too late. Fortunately, a helpful aunt came to Kay's aid just as the reception was beginning.) It is also a good idea to have two or three helpers to assist the person in charge. Look for friends or relatives who want to help, and whom you know to be organized and dependable.

That person's job will be to keep the table filled with food. As soon as a platter or bowl starts looking used up or messy, it should be replaced by a new one. The tray that is removed can be refilled and refreshed in the kitchen.

Make your serving table attractive and professional looking. The difference between your buffet table and an everyday potluck is how the food is presented. Practice ahead of time to see what looks good. You might try elevating the serving bowls and platters by putting them on small boxes weighted with bricks and covered with white linen napkins. Or you might try achieving a "staircase" effect by stacking heavy books on the table and covering them with a tablecloth. Experiment and see what ideas you come up with.

Another attractive and professional trick is to garnish the food trays themselves. You don't need to spend hours carving wedding bells out of radishes or doves out of apples, but do add something. Some possibilities: Decorate the platters with fresh flowers, or with sprigs of parsley or other interesting greens. Or sprinkle the platters with fresh strawberries, melon slices, or pineapple chunks.

Check out the cost of renting plates and glasses versus purchasing plastic. You may be surprised to find that the plastic actually costs more.

If you decide to save money by bringing your own wedding cake to a restaurant reception, be sure to ask if there is a fee to cut the cake. Some places charge between \$.50 and \$3 per person! Obviously it doesn't cost this amount to cut and serve a cake. It's really just a punishment for bringing in your own cake. Ask ahead if there is such a charge, and if so, try to negotiate it away.

You can find recipes for everything from spinach dip to chicken-a-la-king to party punch in recipe books or the recipe boxes of friends or relatives. But we throught we would start out your collection with a recipe for the inexpensive punch we served at Lisa's wedding. It can be made either with or without champagne.

Party Punch

- Powdered fruit drink (or a bottle of fruit drink concentrate or canned fruit punch or frozen lemonade) that will make up 8 quarts
- Vanilla ice cream or fruit-flavored sherbet, half gallon
- Lemon-lime soda, two 2-liter bottles
- Champagne, one bottle (an inexpensive bottle is fine) (For a nice non-alcoholic punch, leave this out.)

Mix the fruit punch in a large punch bowl. At serving time, put spoonsful of ice cream or sherbet into the punch then pour the soda and champagne over it. You will get fifteen quarts of great punch (approximately sixty servings). Be sure to make plenty. Your guests will come back for seconds!

THE WEDDING CAKE

If you order an average-priced tiered wedding cake from a bakery, you can expect to pay between $225 and $400. Actually, cakes are usually priced per person, generally $1 to $4. (In expensive areas, such as Manhattan, the cost can go up as high as $8 per person.) When you are estimating the number of servings, keep in mind that not everyone will eat cake. Ordering for two-thirds of your guests is a more realistic count.

If you are planning to order your cake from a bakery, ask to see real photos of its cakes. Don't settle for the standard pictures in its basic cake book. If a baker says, "Oh, we can make anything you want here," answer, "Great! But I'd still like to see some pictures of cakes you have made."

On the other hand, you don't have to order your cake from a bakery. Here are some options that can save you a considerable amount of money.

A fake cake, approximate cost: $25 to $50.

A fake cake is made out of Styrofoam then frosted to look like a wedding cake. It can be decorated just like a real wedding cake. The cake "layers" are rounds of Styrofoam that can be purchased in craft stores for a dollar or two each. (One layer should be real, however, so that you will have something to cut into when it's time to cut the cake.)

"But," you may ask, "what will my guests eat? Surely not Styrofoam!"

Of course not. You can have homemade sheet cakes in the back that will be cut and served. (The sheet cakes can be baked ahead and stored in friends' freezers until they are ready to frost.) If you don't want to bake the sheet cakes, they can be ordered from a bakery for a lot less money than a wedding cake.

Home bakeries, approximate cost: $50 to $150.

If you would prefer a real cake, consider hiring one of those wonderful bakers who make wedding cakes at home. We have several of them in our town. The woman who baked Lisa's cake offered a wonderful choice of flavors, from poppy seed to chocolate marble to carrot cake. The delicious frosting was a real bonus. It was white and beautiful and held its shape perfectly, yet it didn't taste like shortening. Not a single guest scraped it off, which has to be some kind of a record!

We ordered a modest sized cake, which was decorated with fresh flowers we provided. Then we supplemented it with two sheet cakes, each in a different flavor. Our bill was $50, and we had cake left over.

To find a home baker who does a great job, ask around.

Before you hire anyone, be sure to get references, and don't hesitate to check them.

Buy a supermarket cake, approximate cost: $125 to $200.

If you have never checked wedding cake possibilities and prices at supermarket bakeries, you are sure to be pleasantly surprised. They are certainly worth your consideration. A local supermarket that has its own bakery offers a three-tiered cake that serves up to 125 for $125. A four-tiered cake that serves up to 200 is priced at $170. These cakes can be made in a variety of flavors. The baker says, "Bring in a picture and we will work with you to make exactly what you want for the same price."

You will have to pay extra for a cake top (the selection at some of the supermarkets we checked was quite good) or you can decorate your cake with fresh flowers.

A small wedding cake, plus, approximate cost: $200 to $250.

The larger the cake, the more money you can expect to pay. So a logical way to economize is to buy a smaller cake. To make sure there is enough for all your guests, you can supplement it with those less expensive sheet cakes. Or, again, you can make the sheet cakes yourself and save even more.

One more thing. Many brides like to use a specially decorated knife for the cake cutting. But there is no need to buy one.

Decorate Your Own Cake Knife

You'll be amazed at how simple it is to decorate a
beautiful cake-cutting knife quickly and easily.

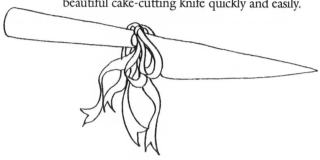

1. Find an inexpensive, long-handled kitchen knife.
2. If the handle of the knife is wood, paint it to match the colors
   you have chosen for your wedding.
3. Decorate the knife with ribbons, bows, flowers, or anything
   that will match your cake table.

To help you plan your own reception, we have included
four worksheets. On the first worksheet, "Reception Theme
Ideas," jot down all your initial thoughts of things you can do
to customize your wedding, to make it truly memorable. This
could include anything from decorations to special family
customs to special entertainment features!

The second is a reception food plan worksheet, and the
third is a worksheet for a do-it-yourself reception. The final
worksheet is an information list for your wedding coordinator.

You did it! Your wedding planning is done! Now you're
ready to start thinking about your honeymoon.

Reception Theme Ideas ❧

_____

_____

_____

_____

_____

_____

_____

_____

_____

_____

_____

_____

_____

_____

_____

_____

_____

_____

_____

_____

_____

_____

_____

Reception Food Plan ✧

Caterer or Contact Person: _____

Phone: _____

Number of Guests: _____ Cost: $ _____

Description of Food:

_____ _____

_____ _____

_____ _____

_____ _____

_____ _____

_____ _____

_____ _____

_____ _____

Beverages:

_____ _____

_____ _____

Equipment Needed:

_____ _____

_____ _____

_____ _____

_____ _____

Do-It-Yourself Reception Planner 🐝

Reception Location: _____

Address: _____

Phone: _____

Time of Day: _____

Contact Person: _____

Phone: _____

Number of Guests: _____

Coordinator: _____

Phone: _____

Necessary Utensils, Serving Items, Appliances

Item Needed	Own	Borrow	Rent	Buy	Source

Volunteers:	Phone

Setup Helpers:	Phone:

Cleanup Helpers:	Phone:

Do-It-Yourself Reception Planner, continued

Food

Dish	Made By	Phone	No. of Servings	Cost

Wedding Coordinator's Reception Information 🐝

Bride:_____

Home Phone:_____ Work Phone:_____

Groom:_____

Home Phone:_____ Work Phone:_____

Wedding Date:_____ Time:_____

Reception Site Contact Person:_____

Phone:_____

Caterer:_____

Arrival Time:_____ Phone:_____

Musicians:_____

_____

Arrival Time:_____ Phone:_____

Helper:_____

Assignment:_____ Phone:_____

Helper:_____

Assignment:_____ Phone:_____

Helper:_____

Assignment:_____ Phone:_____

Helper:_____

Assignment:_____ Phone:_____

Wedding Coordinator's Reception Information, continued

Cleanup Contact Person: _____

Phone: _____

Time Plan

Toasts: _____

Cake Cutting: _____

_____

_____

_____

_____

_____

_____

CHAPTER NINE

The Honeymoon

What is an appropriate honeymoon? A cruise to the Caribbean? A camping trip in the Rockies? A weekend at a lake cottage? A night at a downtown hotel? Regardless of what you read in bridal magazines or what your friends say, the very best honeymoon for you is a time away that both you and your groom would enjoy, and that fits within your budget.

Unfortunately, even the most expensive honeymoon trips can fall short of a couple's expectations. Consider the experiences of two brides, Sandy and Nicole, friends whose weddings were held within weeks of each other.

"Our honeymoon can only be described as a disaster," Sandy says. Why? With all the work there was to be done for the wedding, she and her groom put off planning it until the last minute. When their hastily made reservations fell through less than a week before the big day, they had a huge fight about whose fault the fiasco was. They did go away on their trip, but it cost them almost twice as much as they had planned, and when they came back, they were barely speaking to each other.

Nicole's honeymoon was completely different. "Everyone said we were crazy," she recalls, "but we had the greatest time!" After the wedding and reception, she and her new husband checked into a local hotel and changed into casual clothes. Then they went to McDonald's for a hamburger and french fries, and took in a late movie. The next day they slept until noon, then drove to a picturesque community two hundred miles up the coast where they spent the weekend in a secluded bed and breakfast before driving back in time to be at work on Tuesday. "It might not be right for everyone, but it was perfect for us," Nicole says.

Here, then, are the secrets to a perfect honeymoon: Plan ahead, and do what is most enjoyable to you.

Your honeymoon options are limitless. You might plan a weekend honeymoon, you may decide on a month-long trip, or you may even plan a delayed honeymoon. The latter is especially practical for couples who have children at home, or jobs from which they can't get away. It also is a way to ease the burden on your budget.

Your honeymoon destination should be a place that both you and your groom will enjoy. If it's a place you have never been before, ask for advice and suggestions from people who have been there and who share your views about what is enjoyable. Don't hesitate to ask a lot of questions about where to stay, what activities the place has to offer, where to eat, and what to wear at the time of year you will be there. (When Kay was growing up in San Francisco, she remembers laughing at all the honeymooners who came in summer shorts and sleeveless dresses, and shivered throughout their stay!)

Contact the Chamber of Commerce or get books from automobile associations to help you find out in advance what there is to do and how much things will cost. Are there free festivals in which you can participate? (In Santa Barbara, ethnic festivals are held periodically throughout the year, from French to Irish to Swedish to Greek to Mexican.) Are there outdoor concerts or art shows along the beach? How about free museums and historic sites? Are things close enough to walk? If not, is there good public transportation available? It may be worth joining the American Automobile Association just for the vast amount of free information they make available to their members.

Here are three categories of honeymoons for you to consider: lowest cost, medium priced, and first class on a budget. As we said, the possibilities are endless, but this will give you a starting point. You can take it from there.

LOWEST COST (as low as $100!)

Even if you have next to nothing set aside for a honeymoon, you can still have a getaway to remember. Some ideas:

Enjoy your own city. Most people never really get around to enjoying their own area. If you live in a large, interesting city like Chicago, Atlanta, San Francisco, or Dallas, there are undoubtedly endless opportunities—many of them free or low cost—you could enjoy. (One newly married couple from San Diego paid their first visit to the nationally renowned Old Globe Theater in that beautiful city on their honeymoon. Another from New Orleans spent two days doing their first touristing in the old French quarter.) You can stay in your new apartment or house, and use it as your base of operations.

Take a camping vacation. For couples who love the outdoors, this can be a relaxing, low-cost option. If you don't have the camping equipment you need, start asking around to see what you can borrow.

Loaner homes or cabins. Does anyone in your family, or among your circle of friends, have a lakeside cottage, a mountain retreat, a vacation cabin, or condo you might use?

Let them know you are interested. We know of a newly married couple who stayed at a friend's apartment in a tourist-type town with the mountains and lake close by, and a swimming pool surrounded by pine trees practically outside their back door. And their friend, who was away on vacation, was happy to have free "house sitters."

MEDIUM PRICED (as low as $350 for a weekend)

There are many possibilities here. If you drive rather than fly, stay in medium-priced motels, and eat in inexpensive restaurants, you can keep the cost of many types of trips under control. The main thing is to be sure to plan ahead, and to commit yourself to staying within the amount you budget for each item (no more than $45 a night for a motel room, for instance, or a maximum of $40 a day for food). When you know the cost per day you will allow yourself, divide your total honeymoon budget by that amount to see how many days you will be able to afford to be away.

Here are a couple of other medium price ideas:

Drive a motor home. You will save a lot by not having to pay for lodging, and by being able to prepare some of your own meals. If you have a friend or relative with a motor home you can borrow, great. If not, check to see what is for rent.

More expensive areas with no entertainment costs. You can afford to spend a little more on accommodations and meals if you have no entertainment costs. For instance, one couple spent a weekend in a nice Malibu, California, hotel for $90 a night. Their oceanfront room had a private courtyard where they enjoyed several nice picnics. They spent their days walking along the renowned Pacific Coast Highway and the Malibu pier, visiting the beach, and poking around the quaint shops they encountered.

FIRST CLASS ON A BUDGET (as low as $1,500)

Even though you are on a budget, you don't have to rule out a week in paradise or a cruise to the Caribbean. This is especially true if you have scrimped elsewhere so that you have more to spend on your wedding trip. Here are some suggestions for getting more than your money's worth:

Hawaii. That's right. You might well be able to enjoy those waving palm trees and fragrant ginger blossoms as you sit with your new husband watching the waves roll up on the beach. How, you ask? With Hawaiian holiday packages. These packages include air fare, accommodations, and a number of other perks for about the same price you would normally pay for air fare alone.

Travel agents have access to more than one hundred companies that offer Hawaiian packages. But before you plunk down your money or give the number for your credit card, figure out the exact value of everything you will be getting in the package. You want to be sure that you are indeed getting a good deal.

For more information, contact a travel agent directly, or call Pleasant Holidays toll free at 1-800-2-HAWAII.

Another organization that offers Hawaiian package deals is Creative Leisure. They include discounted rates for a number of luxury Hawaiian hotels. As of this writing, seven-night packages start at $624 per person. Besides a studio apartment complete with a kitchenette, the price includes round trip air fare from San Francisco, and a rental car with unlimited miles. (From New York the cost is $872 per person, and from Chicago it is $928.) You can get a brochure by calling 1-800-426-6367. You can book Creative Leisure packages through a travel agent.

Cruise. Does lazing away tranquil afternoons on a sunny deck after a morning of activities, enjoying tables of luscious food, exploring tropical islands, and snuggling together to watch the sunset appeal to you? Then you may want to consider a cruise. No, cruises are no longer only for the rich. Now they are more affordable than ever.

One warning: Don't listen to people who tell you you'll get the best deal if you wait to book until the last minute. That used to be true, but now most major lines offer their lowest prices to those who book early. (Still, some lines, such as Princess and Costa, do offer two-for-the-price-of-one deals to fill their ships at the last minute, so if you have that flexibility it doesn't hurt to check.)

To get the lowest prices, work with a travel agency that specializes in cruises. They often can get you bargain-basement rates that are not available directly to the public, or even to agents who do a more limited cruise business. A spokesman for one such agency advises, "Don't ever, ever pay brochure rates for a cruise!"

World Wide Cruise Inc. states that their agents can find you a cruise at half price if you are flexible about when you go, which ship you are booked on, and which cabin you get. For more information, call them at 1-800-882-9000.

The Cruise Line, Inc., which advertises savings up to 50 percent off a ship's published rates, can be contacted at 1-800-777-0707.

For a list of travel agencies in your area that specialize in cruises, send a stamped, self-addressed envelope to National Association of Cruise-Only Agencies (NACOA), 3191 Coral Way, Suite 630, Miami, Florida 33145. For more information, you can call them at 305-446-7732.

A budget hint: Cruise lines do have their busy seasons and their off seasons. Many are desperate for passengers during the fall. One travel agent insists many companies will do just about anything to fill their ships during those off months. "I can offer savings up to 70 percent between September and

December," he tells us. If you are getting married in the fall and want a cruise honeymoon, this could be perfect for you. Or you may want to postpone your wedding trip until the less expensive fall months.

TAILOR YOUR HONEYMOON TO YOU

Luxury accommodations on an isolated island, a quiet cottage with a fireplace and piles of good books, a large city with museums and theaters and sites to see, a mountain stream where the trout are plentiful and the scenery is glorious, a leisurely cruise in exotic waters. They are all wonderful ideas, and are all possible, but they are not all right for you. The honeymoon you plan should be:

- Restful and relaxing
- Enjoyable to both of you
- Affordable within your budget
- Workable within the time available to you

With these ideas in mind, use the Honeymoon Priorities chart to help you come up with a honeymoon plan that is just right for you. Then fill out the Honeymoon Itinerary worksheet. You will also want to be collecting brochures, price lists, and so forth.

Happy honeymooning!

Our Honeymoon Priorities ✛

Budget _____

Our honeymoon should be: *(circle all that apply)*

Luxurious   Quiet
Isolated   In a big city
Full of culture Affordable
In the wilderness

_____

_____

We like to: *(circle all that apply)*

Camp   Sightsee
Sunbathe   Sail
Hike   Ski

_____

_____

A perfect local honeymoon would be: _____

_____

A perfect weekend honeymoon would be: _____

_____

A perfect one-week honeymoon would be: _____

_____

A perfect two-week honeymoon would be: _____

_____

A perfect luxury honeymoon would be: _____

_____

Honeymoon Itinerary ✤

Travel Agency: _____

Contact Person: _____ Phone: _____

Honeymoon Dates: from _____ to_____

Wedding Night

Place: _____

Address: _____

Accommodations: _____

Reservations: made _____ confirmed _____ paid _____

Reservations

Travel (Mode)	Phone	Rate	Date	Confirmed

Accommodations (Address)	Phone	Rate	Date	Confirmed

CHAPTER TEN

Afterwards

When the wedding is over and your honeymoon clothes have been hung back in your closet, all those budget concerns will finally be over, right?

Wrong. That's when your budget concerns will really begin. That's the bad news. The good news is that since you have become so good at budget-making, you are way ahead of most couples when it comes to putting together a long-term budget to live on.

But before we get to long-term budgeting, let's talk about some other things you can do to make the most of your money.

FINISH UP THOSE THANK-YOU NOTES

If you have been writing thank-you notes as each gift arrives, this will not be such a big job. If not, take some time to look back at your wedding gift list, then get to work on those thank-yous. The longer you delay, the more likely it is that you will get a gift separated from its card ("Who *gave* us this silver salt and pepper shaker set?" "Are you sure the cookbook was from Aunt Elsie? I thought your sister gave it to us."). Also the greater the chance that you will experience the embarrassment of having someone call you and say, "Did you ever get the gift I sent? Since I haven't heard from you...."

Resist the temptation to resort to printed form thank-you notes with a generic message such as: "Thank you for the beautiful wedding gift. It was exactly what we needed." This is just one cut above no thank-you note at all! You really owe the effort of writing a warm thank-you note to the people who took so much time to choose a gift for you. (Yes, even if the gift wasn't what you had in mind.) In your note, identify the gift, then add a few personal comments. ("Thank you for the lovely brass picture frame. It will look nice on our bedroom dresser. We so appreciate you coming all the way from Kansas for the wedding. I was glad to have the chance to introduce you to Frank. Thank you again for the nice gift. We will enjoy it for years to come.")

It's right here, with your wedding gifts, that you can start making the most of what you have.

EXCHANGING GIFTS

Three toasters when you didn't even need one? Six sets of towels in every color of the rainbow except the sky blue you have chosen for your bath accessories? An elegant, expensive crystal picture frame that just is not you? A clock that plays "Someday My Prince Will Come"? Every couple gets wedding gifts they can't use. Some store them away in boxes, or lug them along as they move from place to place. Others pass them on to other people as gifts. We suggest that you organize your unneeded gifts and exchange as many as possible for things you like and can use. Our best word of advice here is: *Don't put it off!* The longer you wait, the less chance there is that you will be able to successfully exchange everything.

The Gift Exchange chart will help you organize your unneeded gifts and get them ready for exchange.

Gift Exchanges 🐝

We Don't Need	Approximate Value	Where to Exchange

We Still Need	Approximate Value	Where to Exchange

SPENDING YOUR GIFT MONEY

Most couples, when they count up the gift money they received at their weddings, make wonderful plans for it. But many end up using a little to help pay the rent, some more for a special dinner out, a bit more here, a bit more there. The first thing they know, their wedding money is gone and they have nothing to show for it.

Wouldn't you prefer your wedding money to go toward the things you want for your new home? Start by making a comprehensive list of the things you need and want. We have included a checklist to help you determine the things you want to put on your list.

We know we have probably listed things you don't need, especially if you have been married before or if you are already set up in a home. And there will undoubtedly be a number of things you want that are not on this list. Use this as a starting point, then to go on from there.

Now look over your list again with your husband. To which item(s) would you most like to apply your wedding money? Do the two of you agree? You may have to do some discussing between you ("The aerobic steps are more important than an ice fishing hut!"), maybe even some compromising ("OK, OK. We'll put the money toward a vacuum cleaner."). But keep working at it until you can agree on where your wedding money should go. If there isn't quite enough for that specific purchase, put the money in an account and add to it regularly until you can make the purchase.

MAKE A FAMILY BUDGET

Unlike your wedding dress and flowers and cake that are beautiful but are over and done with once your wedding day is past, the budget you and your new husband set up together

For Your New Home ✤

Bedroom

Item	Qty.	Have	Buy New	Donation	Garage Sale	Second-hand
Mattress						
Bed Frame						
Headboard/Footboard						
Dresser						
Nightstand						
Armoire						
Cedar Chest						
Lamps						
Bookcase						
Mirror						
Artwork/Posters						

Second Bedroom/Study

Item	Qty.	Have	Buy New	Donation	Garage Sale	Second-hand
Sofa Bed or Futon						
Desk						
Desk Chair						
Lamp Table						
Chest						
Computer Desk						
Wall Unit						
Bookcase						
Lamp						
Artwork/Posters						
Rugs						

For Your New Home, continued

Dining Room/Kitchen

Item	Qty.	Have	Buy New	Donation	Garage Sale	Second-hand
Table/Chairs						
Hutch						
Corner Cabinet						
Lamps						
Artwork/Posters						

Living Room

Item	Qty.	Have	Buy New	Donation	Garage Sale	Second-hand
Sofa						
Love Seat						
Chair						
Ottoman						
Lamp Table						
Wall Unit						
Coffee Table						
Entertainment Center						
Lamps						
Artwork/Posters						
Rugs						

Special Interests/Recreation

Item	Cost	Item	Cost
Television			
VCR			
Stereo System			
Sports Equipment			
Pets			
Garden			
Workshop			

can set the stage for financial responsibility for the rest of your lives. Allow yourselves enough time to set up your budget thoughtfully and realistically, and to personalize it to specifically fit your own needs.

Are you blending the budgets of two established households? Are there areas of spending on which the two of you have differences of opinion? Do you agree on the need for a savings plan? Are there children to support from previous marriages? Are there old debts that need to be reckoned with? These are some of the things you will need to hammer out together.

It's easy to put off establishing a budget by saying, "Oh, the money will work out all right. Anyway, every time we try to talk about it we just end up arguing."

Don't be fooled. The sooner you work out a budget together, the less you will have to deal with financial problems down the line. There is no better way to invest your time right here at the beginning.

To help you get started, we have put together a basic budget list, on page 215.

Your budget does not have to be set in concrete. But the indisputable rule of economics is that for every dollar you add to one category, a dollar has to be subtracted from another. Make it a rule, right from the beginning, that you will not outspend your income.

A FINAL WORD

You've done it! You have planned the wedding of your dreams at a price you can afford. And you have a master plan to help you put it together from start to finish. From now to your wedding day, keep this book close at hand. When you see pictures of dresses or cakes or flower arrangements you like, cut them out and stick them in. When a good idea for your reception or ceremony or honeymoon occurs to you, jot it down. When you see brochures or price lists or budget plans, put them in, too.

One thing we know—your wedding *will* be wonderful. And you will have done it within your budget.

Congratulations!

The Family Budget ❧

We'll get you started with a list of common expenses for married couples. Be sure to add any extras that you may think of. Begin by filling in estimated monthly amounts for each category. Make it a priority to stay within those amounts each month. If you find that it is impossible, adjust your budget more realistically, but remember, your bottom line cannot exceed what you earn.

Expense	Budgeted Monthly	Actually Spent
Mortgage/rent		
Property tax		
Health care		
Health insurance		
Groceries		
Clothes		
Utilities		
Phone		
Trash removal		
Cable TV		
Gasoline		
Car maintenance		
Car repairs		
Car insurance		
Child care		
Newspaper		
Haircuts		
Restaurants		
Pets		
Entertainment		
TOTAL		

Bibliography

Clark, Beverly. *Planning a Wedding to Remember.* Wilshire Publications: Carpinteria, CA, 1986.

Clark, Leta W. *Affordable Weddings.* Simon & Schuster: New York, 1988.

Gilbert, Edith. *The Complete Wedding Planner.* Fell Publishers: Hollywood, FL, 1989.

Muzzy, Ruth and Hughes, R. Kent. *The Christian Wedding Planner.* Tyndale House: Wheaton, IL, 1991.

Slauson, Judith. *The Second Wedding Handbook.* Doubleday: New York, 1989.

Vanburen, Abigail. *Dear Abby on Planning Your Wedding.* Andrews and McMeel: New York, 1988.

Warner, Diane. *How to Have a Big Wedding on a Small Budget.* Writer's Digest Books: Cincinnati, OH, 1990.

The Family Budget ✣

We'll get you started with a list of common expenses for married couples. Be sure to add any extras that you may think of. Begin by filling in estimated monthly amounts for each category. Make it a priority to stay within those amounts each month. If you find that it is impossible, adjust your budget more realistically, but remember, your bottom line cannot exceed what you earn.

Expense	Budgeted Monthly	Actually Spent
Mortgage/rent		
Property tax		
Health care		
Health insurance		
Groceries		
Clothes		
Utilities		
Phone		
Trash removal		
Cable TV		
Gasoline		
Car maintenance		
Car repairs		
Car insurance		
Child care		
Newspaper		
Haircuts		
Restaurants		
Pets		
Entertainment		
TOTAL		